COMMUNITY ENGAGEMENT IN HOUSING-LED REGENERATION – A GOOD PRACTICE GUIDE

SAM LISTER
JOHN PERRY
MARILYN THORNLEY

PUBLISHED BY THE
CHARTERED INSTITUTE OF HOUSING

The Chartered Institute of Housing

The Chartered Institute of Housing is the professional organisation for people who work in housing. Its purpose is to maximise the contribution housing professionals make to the wellbeing of communities. The Chartered Institute has over 20,000 members across the UK and the Asian Pacific working in a range of organisations – including housing associations, local authorities, arms length management organisations, the private sector and educational institutions.

Chartered Institute of Housing
Octavia House, Westwood Way
Coventry CV4 8JP
Telephone: 024 7685 1700
www.cih.org

TPAS

TPAS, a landlord and tenant group membership organisation, is the leading national tenant participation organisation working to promote tenant empowerment. Its aim is to extend the reach and quality of tenant influence in decision making by contributing to the tenant empowerment agenda with the CLG and Housing Corporation, by working with social housing residents and landlords to develop successful partnerships, and by supporting tenants and community groups to take on a more representative role.

TPAS Ltd, 5th Floor, Trafford House, Chester Road
Manchester, M32 0RS
Telephone: 0161 868 3500
www.tpas.org.uk

Community engagement in housing-led regeneration – a good practice guide
Sam Lister, John Perry, Marilyn Thornley

© Chartered Institute of Housing 2007
Published by the Chartered Institute of Housing
ISBN 978-1-905018-52-9

Graphic design by Jeremy Spencer
Cover photograph by Alex Bramwell/Bigwhitebox.com

Contents

Acknowledgements

The authors of the guide wish to thank their colleagues in CIH and TPAS, particularly Merron Simpson from CIH who has been involved from the outset.

We also thank the advisory group for the guide, whose members were:

Peter Bailey	Government Office for the North West
Hardial Bhogal	RENEW North Staffordshire
David Briscoe	English Partnerships
Ed Ferrari	University of Sheffield
Peter Flynn	New Heartlands
Jacqui Gay	Gateway
Dawn Kehoe	New Heartlands
Ruth Marshall	CLG
Phil Morgan	TPAS
Lester Posner	CLG
Jane Simmonds	CLG
Sally Thomas	Social Regeneration Consultants
Donald Urquhart	English Partnerships
Caroline Williams	CLG

Work on the guide was sponsored jointly by the Department for Communities and Local Government (CLG) and English Partnerships (CLG took over the responsibilities of the former Office of the Deputy Prime Minister on 5 May 2005). English Partnerships is the national regeneration agency helping the government to support high quality sustainable growth in England.

We also received helpful comments on the work from various people in national organisations.

A total of five focus groups with residents were held in different housing market renewal pathfinder areas, to obtain resident views on issues explored in the guide. We are grateful to all the residents who gave their time for these discussions

Our main thanks must go to the dozens of people working in the nine pathfinders or their partner organisations who gave up their time to meet us, arrange visits to individual areas and supply further information that we requested. Their contributions have made the guide possible.

Sam Lister
John Perry
Marilyn Thornley

June 2007

CHAPTER 1

ABOUT THIS GUIDE

Why is the guide needed?

Regeneration of housing areas is taking place in a variety of contexts – for example through national programmes such as New Deal for Communities, and through locally-led initiatives by social landlords which have a strong regeneration focus. At present, however, there is no good practice guidance to community engagement which is specific to housing-led regeneration.

One of the main examples of such regeneration is the housing market renewal (HMR) programme, and its nine regionally-based pathfinders. The pathfinders have a considerable task of restructuring housing markets in their areas so that they relate better to current and expected future demands. It was crucial for many reasons – not least the development of renewed confidence in the future of areas which have been in decline – that residents were brought into the process at an early stage.

Because the HMR programme is intended to make a significant impact in areas which have often experienced decades of housing market problems and wider economic change, it inevitably involves some difficult decisions about the future of those areas and their communities. This makes the task of engaging with those communities both particularly important and – if it is to reach as many as possible of those concerned – an enormous challenge.

Communities need to feel as much a part of the regeneration process as is practicable. They need to have confidence in the arrangements for consulting and advising them on detailed proposals, for keeping them informed as proposals develop and for helping them through the changes that the programmes will set in motion. They need to be assured about the ability of agencies to deliver the planned actions competently.

Many of the features of the HMR programme also occur in other housing-led regeneration projects. Indeed, HMR is such a wide-ranging programme that it can be said to embrace most, if not all, of the circumstances that also face other regeneration projects. It is also part of its purpose to provide wider lessons for housing-led regeneration.

This guide therefore uses the experience of the HMR programme to set out wide-ranging guidance that can apply to housing-led regeneration more generally.

What does the guide aim to do?

The guide aims to help housing and regeneration practitioners in their task of engaging with the local communities in the areas they cover. Although its examples are mainly drawn from the HMR pathfinders, which have particular characteristics of delivering large-scale regeneration programmes within relatively short periods of time, it is also intended to apply in other situations where housing areas are going through comprehensive regeneration, led by local authorities, housing associations and others.

The aim of the guide is threefold:
- to identify the key stages, in preparing and implementing a strategy for regeneration, at which practitioners need to engage with local communities
- to set down practical approaches to doing so, using examples from the HMR pathfinders, or from regeneration projects elsewhere, that provide relevant lessons, and
- to propose standards about engaging with communities that can be applied both at strategic level and the level of decision-making about individual neighbourhoods, streets and homes, and show how they might be used.

We therefore make considerable use of the experiences of HMR – making sure that these are available to and shared by other practitioners – and try to bring to their activities a detached view which helps to bring out lessons which others can make use of in taking forward regeneration projects.

Who is the guide for?

The guide is aimed at all those agencies concerned with housing-led regeneration, such as local authorities or housing associations. The guide is also aimed at residents in regeneration areas, their community organisations, representatives and people working with them. We hope that it may also be useful to those concerned about the impact of regeneration on communities – such as local politicians, the media and others.

The guide is specific to the legislation and policy context in England, although its broader messages are relevant to the rest of the UK.[1]

How was the guide prepared?

Sources for the guide are as follows:

- visits to and discussions with senior staff in all nine HMR pathfinder areas, and consideration of follow up material provided as a result of these interviews
- focus groups with residents carried out in five of the pathfinder areas
- a review of literature about housing-led regeneration
- consideration of practical examples from other regeneration programmes
- informal discussions with the CLG, the Audit Commission, and a range of practitioners and organisations engaged in housing-led regeneration.

The authors of the guide also had background experience in strategic housing issues, housing renewal, resident participation and housing advice services, all of which are directly relevant to the guide's remit.

The guide was prepared by staff from CIH and TPAS, with assistance from the advisory group and from the CLG staff who commissioned the project in its original form as a web-based guide for HMR practitioners.

How is the guide organised?

The guide is in three parts.

Part one sets the context. Chapter 2 gives the background to the housing market renewal programme for those who are unfamiliar with it or require a refresher on what it involves (practitioners familiar with the programme may want to skip this chapter). Chapter 3 describes different levels and types of community engagement, and the issues and principles that apply.

Part two sets out good practice principles and includes practical examples at the different levels of intervention described in chapter 3. Chapter 4 is about the broad options at the strategic level. Chapters 5 and 6 are about the neighbourhood level. And chapter 7 is about decision-making on individual streets and houses.

---

1   A 'how to' guide to community engagement in regeneration in Scotland is available at http://www.ce.communitiesscotland.gov.uk/stellent/groups/public/documents/webpages/cs_006709. hcsp#P30_1062

Part three then looks in more detail at certain aspects of community involvement which cut across these three levels. Separate, short chapters deal respectively with:

- skills for community engagement
- using consultants and community engagement
- engagement and community cohesion
- formal engagement in the planning process
- community capacity building
- dealing with publicity and the media.

The needs of people who require special care/support (leaseholders, older people, disabled people, BME communities, etc) are not dealt with in a separate chapter but are reflected throughout the guide.

In most chapters there are boxed examples from the pathfinders and elsewhere, and checklists about particular tasks (eg organising public meetings) which are intended to be helpful reminders rather than definitive lists of things to do.

The CIH/TPAS recommended standards for community engagement, referred to at points throughout the guide, are presented in an Annex. These were developed in relation to the HMR programme but can be adapted to any appropriate housing-led regeneration project. There are also links to these standards, at appropriate points, throughout the text.

Terms used in the guide

Most of the terminology used in the guide is either obvious or is explained where it occurs. 'Regeneration agency' is used as a generic term to refer to any body engaged in regeneration. The housing market renewal programme is referred to throughout as 'HMR', and 'pathfinders' are the nine official pathfinder bodies (or the areas they cover). Reference to their 'partners' normally means the constituent local authorities but in some cases means housing associations or arms length management organisations (ALMOs) actively engaged in the programme. In the text, following convention, CLG (Communities and Local Government) is referred to as 'the Department'.

Because not all place names used in the guide will be familiar to all readers, where appropriate they are followed by an abbreviation showing in which pathfinder area they are located. The pathfinder names and the abbreviations are shown in the Table opposite.

Pathfinder (abbreviation used in this guide)	Location
Bridging NewcastleGateshead (BNG)	Newcastle and Gateshead
Elevate East Lancashire (EEL)	East Lancashire
Gateway (GH)	Hull and East Riding
Manchester-Salford Partnership (MSP)	Manchester and Salford
New Heartlands (NH)	Merseyside
Partners in Action (PIA)	Oldham and Rochdale
RENEW North Staffordshire (RNS)	North Staffordshire
Transform South Yorkshire (TSY)	South Yorkshire
Urban Living (UL)	Birmingham and Sandwell

These abbreviations are also used in the text as shorthand for the individual pathfinders.

CHAPTER 2

HOUSING MARKET RENEWAL –
AN EXAMPLE OF REGENERATION

What this chapter is about

- what is housing market renewal
- the pathfinders and how they work
- how does housing market renewal fit in with previous regeneration programmes

Housing market renewal exemplifies many of the elements associated with housing-led regeneration more generally: housing renovation in both public and private sectors, wider area renewal and environmental regeneration, selective redevelopment, improved management of neighbourhoods, regeneration of commercial areas and closer working with communities. This chapter gives a brief overview of the HMR programme, aimed at readers unfamiliar with it. Others may wish to pass directly to chapter 3.

More detailed information on HMR can be found on the Department's web pages[2] and those of the Audit Commission.[3]

The housing market renewal programme

The housing market renewal (HMR) programme is a targeted response to the problems of low or weak housing demand which occur mainly in parts of the north and Midlands. In April 2002 the government announced the creation of nine 'pathfinders', covering areas which account for about half of the incidence of low demand. The boundaries reflect the actual incidence of low demand rather than administrative arrangements: market failure is a sub-regional problem and the pathfinders cover much larger areas than previous area-based renewal programmes.

---

2   www.communities.gov.uk/index.asp?id=1140273
3   www.audit-commission.gov.uk/housing/marketrenewal.asp?CategoryID=english%5E1628&page=
     index.asp&area=hpsector

What primarily distinguishes housing market renewal from earlier regeneration programmes is that it is intended to respond to evidence about housing market change at the sub-regional level. Housing market change has three distinct features:[4]

- *stock obsolescence:* where the character of the stock has been overtaken by consumer preferences and aspirations

- *surplus housing stock:* changes in the economic base (such as a decline in manufacturing) result in an excess of supply

- *unpopular neighbourhoods:* where a number of local factors, such as property design, stigma, crime and anti-social behaviour, interact to deter potential new residents and cause existing residents to want to leave.

Where all three combine, the result is housing market failure – low demand coupled with declining or stagnating house prices. Because each area has its own unique pattern of obsolescent, surplus or unpopular housing, and does not necessarily combine all three, the most appropriate intervention to apply in a particular case will vary from neighbourhood to neighbourhood.

Pathfinder governance and operations

Because pathfinders cover large areas which often cross several local authority boundaries, this affects their governance. Broadly, each pathfinder has a board responsible for the overall strategic direction of the pathfinder and for monitoring performance. There is no single template for the board and the particular arrangements and composition depend on local circumstances. Typically, each board comprises representatives from some or all of the following:

- the statutory authorities (eg local government, health, the police)

- Local Strategic Partnerships

- government agencies (government offices, English Partnerships)

- delivery agencies (eg housing associations, private sector)

- the voluntary and community sectors with an interest in the pathfinder.

Each pathfinder has a core team which is responsible to the board. The functions of the core team vary – but a key role is to provide the delivery teams with specialist and strategic support. Typical core functions include responsibility for developing strategic initiatives and holding particular budgets, research, monitoring and developing guidance.

---

4   Cole, I and Nevin, B (2004), *The Road to Renewal: The early development of the Housing Market Renewal programme in England*, Joseph Rowntree Foundation, York.

Pathfinder prospectuses

Each pathfinder has produced a 'prospectus' which sets out its overall strategy. Other regeneration initiatives may have similar strategic documents. Each prospectus contains:

- data and analysis of the housing market and of the main drivers for housing market change
- the vision for the area
- details about the arrangements for scrutiny and governance
- risk analysis
- monitoring and evaluation
- the approach to consultation
- a description of local level interventions.

A feature of the HMR programme is that it is intended to be flexible enough to adapt to changing housing market conditions. The prospectus is intended to act as a guide to the overall direction of the pathfinder and as a statement of general intent over the medium to long term, rather than as a detailed operational plan. The prospectus also forms the framework for inspection by the Audit Commission, whose recommendations influence each pathfinder's plans.

Funding of the HMR programme

Like many other housing-led regeneration programmes, HMR is predominantly a capital programme. Some revenue expenditure is permitted, for example for set up costs. Some types of revenue expenditure can be converted into a capital cost ('capitalised') – such as professional fees charged by consultants, or where repairs are absorbed into a programme of planned major works. However, because most funding is capital the programme is likely to depend on other funding sources – for example, local authority General Fund expenditure – to finance revenue spending such as that associated with community engagement or with detailed advice to householders.

The pathfinders began implementing their programmes in 2004. An initial advance of £4m from the HMR fund was made to each pathfinder for set up costs and 'quick win' actions – for example, the demolition of unpopular tower blocks, crime reassurance work and research into refugee housing issues (UL). By the end of 2005/06 they had been allocated just under £600m. Current funding extends until March, 2008, and beyond that will depend of the outcome of the Comprehensive Spending Review 2007.

Scrutiny and performance monitoring

In each pathfinder, funding agreements are in place between each of the constituent local authorities and the Department. These agreements set out a range of outputs to be achieved during each funding cycle in the programme. The Department's core outputs contain targets for:

- homes acquired (separate targets for the social and private sector)
- homes demolished (again both sectors)
- land acquired
- homes constructed, refurbished or improved
- homes subject to additional neighbourhood management and environmental work.

Each pathfinder board may also set its own additional output targets.

As well as its independent scrutiny role, the Audit Commission carries out six-monthly monitoring visits. Their monitoring reports are shared with the pathfinder and the Department. The Audit Commission also has a role as 'critical friend' to the HMR programme.

Related regeneration programmes

Of the neighbourhoods covered by the pathfinders which have the worst housing market problems, many have been or are still the subject of other regeneration initiatives. In many cases, this means that residents will have already been involved in community engagement activities of some kind, aimed at shaping these programmes. This has been an important factor for the pathfinders and their partners to take into account in planning work in each neighbourhood.

The unique regeneration history of an area should be taken into account in determining the best approach to community engagement. Within any regeneration programme there may be a number of areas which have their own distinctive histories (eg former General Improvement Areas). An approach that works well in one area may be inappropriate in another, even when the neighbourhoods are adjacent to each other.

See the example on the next page.

History of Burngreave and Fir Vale, Sheffield

Burngreave and Fir Vale are adjacent areas within the wider East Sheffield regeneration area and are the subject of a single masterplan. However, the two areas have rather different regeneration histories and the communities are quite distinct. There is limited cross-community contact. This distinctiveness has been reflected in the approach to consultation and in the overall masterplan which was adopted in May, 2005.

Burngreave is a racially-diverse area in which 23 community languages are spoken. It has a strong tradition of resident activism and radical politics. In the past the area has attracted the lion's share of regeneration funding. Around 50% of the stock is social rented housing. The area is also the subject of a New Deal for Communities programme so there were relatively well-developed community structures already in place.

Fir Vale has a minority white population and is host to one of Sheffield's major Pakistani Muslim communities that comprise 50% of the total population. It also contains significant numbers of people from newer migrant groups, including people from Eastern Europe and North Africa. Prior to HMR, it had virtually no developed community infrastructure – except perhaps around the mosques. There was some resentment that Burngreave seemed to attract all the funding. The majority tenure is owner occupation (about 60%) but with a sizeable private rented sector (about 15%). The first move under the HMR programme was to appoint a community development worker to try to build the community capacity in the area, which (unlike Burngreave) had not gained from previous programmes.

More information: Sheffield City Council's East Sheffield Regeneration Team, 0114 256 2182

CHAPTER 3

ENGAGING WITH COMMUNITIES – GENERAL PRINCIPLES

What this chapter is about

- why engaging with residents is vital to housing-led regeneration
- the kinds of engagement that might be appropriate
- the critical success factors
- special features of the HMR programme that affect engagement with residents

Why engage with communities?

The housing market renewal pathfinders have a considerable task of reconfiguring housing markets in their areas, which they are doing through partnership with local authorities, housing associations, developers and many other stakeholders whose roles are crucial to the success of HMR. Arguably, however, the residents and potential residents of an area are the most important of all the stakeholders in any housing-led regeneration programme. There are several reasons for this:

1. It is residents (and potential residents) who will determine whether an area has a future, because ultimately they will decide if they value living in a particular area or not. Some may 'vote with their feet' by moving into (or out of) an area, others may stay because they are content with an area, or conversely because they find it difficult to leave. Residents' opinions therefore are clearly a key measure – perhaps *the* key measure – of whether the programme is a success.

2. Residents' opinions matter because it is the future of their neighbourhoods and their homes which is at stake. In all nine pathfinder areas, decisions are being taken which affect the future of thousands of individual homes, both rented and owner-

occupied, and the plans should be based on residents' views. Indeed, unless the plans are 'owned' by the majority of residents, they are unlikely to succeed.

3. Regeneration agencies face difficult decisions about the future of areas where houses are in too poor condition or demand is too low for the houses to be retained. In these cases, listening to residents is even more crucial, not only to get the decisions right but to assure politicians and the media that they are based in local opinion. Being able to demonstrate that actions are firmly grounded in what local people think, is the strongest argument that the chosen course of action is the best available. It will also, of course, be of immense benefit in actually carrying the plans through successfully.

4. Finally, residents themselves are a vital source of information about local areas – they are part of the 'evidence base' on which regeneration rests. They provide intelligence and information simply because they are the ones who live there, know the places inside out, and can be a valuable source of ideas about how to make improvements.

As the HMR programme is one that was introduced within the nine pathfinder areas by government, rather than emerging from local demands, it made it particularly important to engage with residents at an early stage so that their influence could begin to be felt. Inevitably this meant explaining and justifying the programme, and showing how the resources available can be used to address needs which are apparent to residents.

These are the key reasons for engaging with communities. Of course, there are others – including the expectations of central and local government and of the Audit Commission, legislative requirements which might apply in some cases, responding to demands from local activists or from the media, and others. However, we suggest that the reasons set out above are – or should be – the main drivers behind resident engagement in housing-led regeneration.

The guide also takes as a premise that community engagement is not an 'add-on' to regeneration but is an essential and integral part of it. Plans and budgets need to allow for the time, the staffing and the costs of engagement at the various levels considered in the guide.

This chapter sets the context for the practical material later in the guide by posing some important general questions about engaging with residents. Why are we doing it (see above)? What do we mean by 'engagement'? What are likely to be the key ingredients for success? And what are the particular features of the pathfinder programme that determine the shape of community engagement in it.

What kinds of engagement are appropriate?

There is a long history to engagement of residents in decision-making in housing and planning issues that does not need to be explained here. Much of it came about in response to protests that residents were *not* involved, particularly in decisions about whether older housing areas should or should not be demolished in the 1960s. The principles about participation in town planning, and practical experience of resident involvement in urban renewal, have their origins in this period and are still relevant to regeneration programmes.

One earlier commentator, still much quoted, suggested that there is a 'ladder' of participation, reflecting different levels of power exercised by communities.[5] However, this kind of analysis implies that the lower 'rungs' on the ladder are less valid or represent only token degrees of engagement. In reality, different kinds of participation are appropriate for different levels of decision-making and at different stages in a project.

For this guide we will discuss five different kinds of participation:[6]

Informing	telling people about regeneration plans, and engaging their interest in them
Consulting	offering people options, getting feedback from them and taking account of their views
Deciding together	encouraging people to develop ideas or options, and giving them some influence in deciding the way forward
Acting together	joint decision-making on action to be taken, and forming partnerships with residents' groups to carry it out
Supporting independent community initiatives	helping residents to carry out their own plans or initiatives – for example by grant-aiding or in other ways supporting them, while leaving them in charge of what happens

In the CIH/TPAS Recommended Standards, standard 2.5 says that the level of engagement should be appropriate to the impact which decisions are likely to have on residents. Examples of these different levels are given throughout the guide.

---

5   Originally put forward in an article by Sherry Arnstein in 1969 (and available with a commentary via http://www.partnershipsonline.org.uk/index.cfm?fuseaction=main.viewBlogEntry&intMTEntryID=2350).
6   This section and the next use and adapt work by David Wilcox and Marilyn Taylor. See Wilcox, D (1994) *Guide to Effective Participation*. JRF, York (out of print, but downloadable at www.partnerships.org.uk), and Taylor, M (1995) *Unleashing the Potential: Bringing residents to the centre of regeneration*. JRF, York. Further references to Wilcox and Taylor relate to these two sources.

What are the critical success factors in engaging with residents?

In a sense, the whole of this guide is about this question, but there are some important general issues, from previous work on this subject, which need to be addressed before looking in detail at how to engage with residents.

Getting known

One of the key early success factors must be the basic one of telling people why the regeneration programme exists and what the agencies involved are doing. Without this, any efforts at deeper engagement will just be a waste of time. Simple messages about who the main agencies are and how they affect people – and getting this across to as many residents as possible – are therefore the starting point for everything that follows.

[Standard 1.1]

Understanding each neighbourhood

Each area or estate is different. As Marilyn Taylor says (see footnote 3):

> '...regeneration strategies need to start from a careful assessment of the nature and history of a particular estate, the factors which shape it, and the resources available to it. In particular, every effort should be made to challenge the stereotyping and prejudice from which many estates suffer. While it is important to acknowledge the pressure under which residents live, it is even more important to recognise the assets and potential that local people, local buildings and local firms and services represent.'

Strategies to engage residents need to be based on an understanding of their circumstances. Of course, this can't be achieved overnight, but it is important that mechanisms are in place to achieve this understanding at local level.

[Standard 1.5]

Sharing power

Much of regeneration is about harnessing the power and resources of various 'stakeholders' to develop and achieve a common goal about regenerating areas that are in decline. But the present and future residents of an area are its biggest asset, and sharing some power with them may also be a way of achieving regeneration goals more readily. If residents themselves have a degree of power over the future of their areas, they are likely to be more committed to the process and more likely to defend what has been achieved. Devolving power in this way is also part of the government's agenda for empowering local communities.[7]

As one resident said in one of the focus groups for the guide:

'We are the community that will have to live here after the improvements, so let us have a major say.'

There must be careful decisions about the circumstances in which power might be shared (not least, to protect the interests of less powerful groups within a community). There are many examples in the guide of power-sharing – for example, involving residents in decision-making on the choice of contractors.

[Standard 2.6]

Sharing information

Information is crucial. Sharing it as early, as fully and as clearly as possible is crucial to building confidence in the relationship between the agencies, their partners and the community. This applies especially to information which may cause disappointment such as reductions in resources and programme delays. 'No news' only provokes mistrust and rumours.

Agencies and their partners also need to communicate clearly with communities about the parameters of what they can do. People understand that resources are limited, and shouldn't be encouraged to build up unrealistic expectations with inevitable disappointment when they can't be met.

[Standard 2.1]

Building commitment

Building commitment is arguably one of regeneration's most important tasks – because if people are committed and have a stake in the future of their area, they are more likely to want to live there and other people are more likely to want to join them. This is basically what all of the HMR pathfinders are setting out to achieve. Building commitment is therefore fundamental to most of the measures discussed in this guide.

People are most likely to be committed if the ideas come from them ('we thought of that') or result from their own views about the problems in their area. This is not

---

7   See the local government white paper: CLG (2006) *Strong and Prosperous Communities*, part 2.

always possible, but it is vital that the ideas respond to residents' analyses of what the problems are and their priorities for solving them. Ideas from elsewhere can often be successful – but this is more likely if residents are able to say 'we've been to see that and it works'. When ideas that come from local communities actually come to fruition, this gives an opportunity to recognise (in some form, like an opening ceremony) the part the community has played.

One particular aim is to get people living in areas needing regeneration to recognise what the issues are and to endorse a vision for changing those areas to give them a new future.

[Standard 1.4]

Reaching the 'non-joiners'

The HMR and other regeneration programmes are operating in areas where there are likely to be many people marginalised within their communities for a variety of reasons – poverty, tenant turnover, elderly people who find it difficult to leave their homes, people whose first language is not English, young people with little interest in public meetings, etc. Measures which involve the whole community, or which target non-joiners or hard-to-reach groups, are therefore particularly important. This is likely to require time, using a variety of methods to engage residents, and being willing to explain things many times as new people arrive in an area.

[Standard 3.2]

Developing residents' confidence and capacity

Inevitably, regeneration programmes are directed at many communities which are run-down, where many former residents may have left and where those that remain may (in some cases) have little confidence in their ability to effect change and limited capacity to be natural 'leaders'.

An important dimension to engagement is therefore building peoples' confidence and capacity. Wilcox says (see footnote 3):

'Ideas and wish lists are little use if they cannot be put into practice. The ability to do that depends as much on people's confidence and skills as it does on money. Many participation processes involve breaking new ground – tackling difficult projects and setting up new forms of organisations.

'It is unrealistic to expect individuals or small groups suddenly to develop the capability to make complex decisions and become involved in major projects.

They need training – or better still the opportunity to learn formally and informally, to develop confidence, and trust in each other.'

[Standard 7.1]

Aiming for lasting change

The HMR programme recognises that change in the prospects for local economies and housing markets will not come overnight but will take a period of several years. The same applies to empowering residents. Taylor argues that:

'Prospects for sustainability will be increased by the development of local capacity, both among residents and in locally-managed mainstream services. But they also depend crucially on developing community-controlled 'successor' bodies with assets, endowments or attractive opportunities for future investment.'

[Standard 7.2]

Being realistic, and having clear limits

However much effort is put into community engagement, it is almost impossible to close the 'gap' between the way that those in authority see events, and how they are seen by residents. The aim is to narrow this gap, not necessarily to close it completely. Some residents may not consider their views have been taken into account unless they get exactly what they asked for, which is not always feasible. Most residents though should, as a result of the work done, feel reasonably satisfied with how their views have been taken into account. If surveys or wider signs of discontent show that this is not the case, action needs to be taken. Having involvement of a third party to whom residents can have recourse, having independent evaluation of community engagement, and above all having locally-based staff who are known and trusted by most residents, are all ways of closing the gap (and examples will follow in the detailed chapters).

At the same time, engagement is bound to take place within certain boundaries – that will vary from issue to issue, from neighbourhood to neighbourhood, and during the life of the programme. Those leading the engagement should be clear beforehand what the limits are – and convey these to residents in appropriate ways. Trying to engage everyone on every issue simply raises expectations that cannot then be met.

[Standard 2.2]

These elements of what successful 'engagement' might involve will be referred to in looking at examples later in the guide – those that help to achieve them will be of particular interest. They will also be relevant when we look in chapter 4 at how agencies measure success in engaging residents.

What special features of the HMR programme affect engagement with residents?

The HMR programme represents a particular approach to housing-led regeneration which has distinct features. What are these and how should they be taken into account in what we say about relationships with residents?

Pathfinders are engaged in a common task and are at similar stages to each other

Although there are many differences between pathfinders, their broad agenda is a shared one and they are at similar stages. Interchanges between residents' groups in the different areas may therefore be a powerful way of getting people to take responsibility for the ideas about what should be done, as well as helping to build their own confidence and capacity.

Pathfinders operate at different levels within large geographical areas

Pathfinders usually cover more than one local authority area, deal with perhaps 100,000+ households and have to engage with many different estates and neighbourhoods. For convenience, the guide considers three levels of operation – the overall strategy for an area (such as a pathfinder area), decisions on the future of particular neighbourhoods or estates, and decisions on individual properties. (This is an oversimplification. But it helps to bring out overall principles that can be adapted to local circumstances.)

It is general experience that it is easier to get residents to engage with decisions at the level of their neighbourhood – and even more so with decisions that affect their own home – than in strategy covering broader areas. Nevertheless, the aim of 'getting known' must apply across the pathfinder areas, while the more ambitious success factors about resident engagement are likely to apply mainly at local levels. There are opportunities though for resident contact across the pathfinder area to exchange ideas and experiences.

Pathfinders have an unusual role

Pathfinder status can be confusing. Are they part of local government? Or a private sector body? Communicating their role can be difficult, and pathfinders have to be sensitive about the role of the local authority (in particular) as the democratically-elected body to which residents might normally relate. In certain areas other bodies (eg housing associations or ALMOs, as landlords) will also have their own engagement mechanisms.

This means that almost any engagement must be *in partnership* with the local authority and perhaps other bodies, and the roles of each must be constantly (and consistently) explained.

It also makes it especially important to engage with elected members in the local authorities, if possible securing them as allies of HMR rather than having them as opponents. Particular efforts need to be made to keep them informed, to educate them about the process and to involve them in decision-making on their 'patch' (the guide has various examples where this has been done). As one practitioner commented: 'engage politicians and get political support before you even get near communities'.

Pathfinders may follow other programmes

Virtually all of the nine pathfinders were set up in areas where there was already a history of regeneration activity, past renewal programmes and varied measures to engage local communities. The history of these processes, the structures they have created and the changes they have brought all need to be taken into account – although old arrangements are not set in stone and may well need to be adapted to the new circumstances.

There is also the ever-present danger of 'consultation fatigue' – residents having been exposed to too many consultation processes, perhaps in some cases with little tangible outcome – that needs to be taken into account in planning fresh engagement initiatives.

Pathfinders are time-limited

As in other regeneration programmes, the long-term role of maintaining the viability of areas will fall to the local authorities responsible for the area, and to the communities themselves. The pathfinders must always have in mind an 'exit' or 'handover' strategy for when this eventually happens – and aim to leave strong relationships in place that do not depend on a programme that has a limited life. Part of this must involve the pathfinders being 'learning' organisations – and being able to pass the learning on to their partners.

Pathfinders are dependent on availability of long-term funding

As with the previous point, HMR has similarities to other regeneration programmes which are trying to achieve long-term change through specially-created, short-life agencies. In the case of the pathfinders this is combined with the enormous scale of their areas, and having programmes which (because of factors like having to acquire land) stretch over many years.

These features make the task of engaging with residents especially demanding. Pathfinders or their partners often need to be able to make promises to residents that will not come to fruition for 2-3 years or perhaps more. They are therefore even more dependent on long-term funding than are other regeneration programmes. Getting residents to understand this and accept setbacks if resources do not materialise is a particular challenge.

What are the key features of other housing-led regeneration projects?

A similar analysis needs to be carried out of any regeneration initiative, asking similar questions about how the nature of the programme and the way it came about affect the task of engaging with communities. What particular features of the project or programme need to be taken into account in deciding the approach to community engagement?

CHAPTER 4

ENGAGING AT STRATEGIC LEVEL

What this chapter is about

- why engagement at strategic level is important
- the kinds of engagement that might be appropriate
- practical examples of each
- problems that arise
- advantages and disadvantages

Why consider community engagement at strategic level?

At first sight it might seem reasonable to start to consider community engagement only at the level of the neighbourhood – or lower. However, in chapter 3 the guide set out the main reasons why engagement in housing-led regeneration is of particular importance, and the first came from the HMR programme – the aim of 'turning around' the housing markets in the pathfinder areas. Clearly, decisions by individual householders to stay or leave, to buy or rent houses or to sell them or move out, are key to this. If residents and potential residents feel a degree of 'ownership' of the regeneration programme, and confidence that it is working in their interests, they are more likely to be committed to staying in or interested in moving to the area.

At strategic level, there is the considerable challenge of encouraging people to engage with broad issues and overcome a normal lack of interest in things that may not appear to relate directly to their homes or neighbourhoods. This challenge makes community engagement at strategic level both more necessary and more difficult to achieve and sustain.

What issues should be decided at strategic level?

There are several issues that can most appropriately be decided at strategic level. Those covered in this chapter are:

1. ways of 'getting the message across' – about what the lead agency is, what it does, how it relates to other bodies and what impact it is having

2. how to involve residents in setting strategic goals and priorities

3. standards for community engagement that will apply across the area and across the activities of different agencies

4. ensuring that communications aimed at residents are readily understandable

5. priorities between areas, and the level of resources for engagement work available and over what timescales

6. how to ensure consistency – in messages from the different agencies, and in treatment of different parts of the area

7. ways of recognising community initiatives, and of building capacity within communities – so that they can develop their own 'voices' and start to shape their communities themselves

8. how to judge the overall effectiveness of engagement at strategic level

9. how to learn from engagement, linking it to what went before and what will follow.

The rest of the chapter addresses these nine themes, considers different approaches, gives examples and offers good practice advice. While the discussion is based on engagement at the level of the HMR pathfinder, many of the points made or examples given apply equally in other contexts, eg looking at the future of several neighbourhoods in one inner city area when deciding regeneration priorities.

1. How does the regeneration agency get its image across?

In the HMR programme, as in other regeneration programmes, the lead agency has continually to reinforce its image among residents, remind them what it is doing, publicise and gain recognition for its successes and – as far as possible – earn and maintain residents' support.

Because of the nature of the areas and the issues, two groups of people are of particular importance – new residents and potential residents. HMR aims to stabilise housing markets, so potential 'movers', whether 'in' or 'out', are as much a target group as longer-standing residents. Understanding their motives, getting across the message about the programme and – as far as possible – engaging with them alongside other residents, are all important tasks. Experience in regeneration generally shows that an area's reputation may improve very slowly with outsiders, even if the area has been transformed: positive publicity can therefore be important in accelerating reputational change.[8]

The basic range of methods for establishing and conveying an agency's image is fairly obvious – a recognisable logo and other clear and attractive branding, using media such as newsletters, a website, and so on, and using other local or regional media via press releases, show houses, staged publicity events, etc.

[Standard 1.1]

2. How do agencies engage with residents in setting their overall goals and priorities?

It is difficult to engage residents in setting goals and priorities, which may often seem vague, wide-ranging and not relevant to their own problems. In addition, agencies may have a hostile reception and may have to overcome perceptions that areas have been neglected. Changing this into positive discussions about the future can be challenging. Examples of such negativity come from a non-pathfinder study (below).

Negative responses from initial engagement in a new regeneration project

This example is from a local authority undertaking an HMR-style approach to its older areas. A community engagement exercise initially produced the following negative responses:

- many people are angry about the rapid decline of their once stable communities and often blame the council and private landlords for their plight
- people are generally unhappy about the prospect of radical change, particularly large-scale demolition, often feeling that the problem is one of 'people, not buildings'
- they feel that refurbishment options are preferable, for a variety of reasons, and want to see early action on anti-social behaviour, crime and environmental services
- some people feel their neighbourhoods have reached a point where radical change is now the only way forward, welcome the prospect of early rehousing, but are worried about when and how it will be achieved, how they will cope and the financial impact on their usually limited household budgets

→

---

8   A study looking at challenging unpopular images of three estates is Dean, J and Hastings, A (2000) *Challenging Images – Housing estates, stigma and deprivation*. JRF, York.

- many people want to keep their communities together, but some see housing market renewal as a threat to their established networks and way of life

People's views on these crucial issues do change over time, as understanding increases, people are fully engaged, and trust is built between community groups and delivery bodies.

Source: a report on one area by Social Regeneration Consultants.

As the report on this example goes on to say:

'Engaging with communities in these circumstances is fraught with difficulties. But it is no less important for that. People need to understand the background to housing market renewal programmes and the reasons why change is needed. They need to make an informed choice about the best way forward, for themselves and their community and in the long term, not just the next year or two. And they need to feel that their input is making a real difference.'

In the HMR context, this indicates a need to engage residents in discussing the reasons for the programme, why their areas were included, the consequences of inaction, the scope of the HMR programme (its resources and timescale) and the scope for communities to become engaged.

Bearing the nature of this task in mind, it is worth considering using several different methods for engaging residents. Here we consider methods in which small numbers of residents are brought into the process in more depth, and are encouraged to 'own' the programme and (when appropriate) act as advocates for it – as well as those which involve collecting views very widely across the pathfinder area.

Engaging with small numbers of residents – board membership and residents' consultative committees

One way of doing this is to incorporate resident members into the regeneration board, or into other elements of the governance arrangements. Some pathfinders have done this as a way of ensuring resident involvement in key decisions about the pathfinder, but it has limitations. One is the usual one which applies to board members which is that they are there to exercise a governance duty, just like the other board members, rather than to represent a particular interest (although this does not, of course, mean that they do not bring a resident 'perspective' to the board, indeed that is one reason for having them). Another difficulty (which has occurred in the context of tenant board members of ALMOs and HAs) is the possibility of a gap opening up between the views of resident board members and residents generally, as the former become more and more involved in governance.

A variant of this method is to have an advisory board of residents which reports to the main board – though this may have the disadvantages of resident board members without strong advantages. Nevertheless it is an approach used in some areas and which may be appropriate, especially as a way of bringing together representatives from different residents' groups across the regeneration area.

[Standard 1.7]

Engaging with small numbers of residents – other methods

'Citizens' juries' or 'citizens' panels' are methods for engaging residents in setting goals and priorities without directly involving them in governance arrangements. They can be thought of as a form of focus group, but instead of being convened on a 'one-off' basis, a group of residents is brought together for familiarisation with (or training on) the issues, prior to substantive discussion. The group may also be asked to reconvene periodically to feed into strategic decisions (PIA have done this). Another way of doing the same thing in a more concentrated format is to have a one-day workshop.

Here is a checklist for such methods, which could of course be used for parts of the regeneration area as well as for the whole. However, at neighbourhood level (see chapter 5), it is much more likely that regular meetings will take place with a locally-representative group.

Checklist for citizens' juries, panels or workshops

✓ is an experienced facilitator available?

✓ is he/she well briefed on what you want to get out of it, and likely to be seen as trusted and independent?

✓ are those invited as representative as possible of different areas and groups?

✓ do you need an incentive to get people to attend, eg travel expenses?

✓ what materials will you need? – will the event be informative and lively?

✓ how will you deal with negative comments that arise, and move people on to making positive ones?

✓ how will you make sure you get the everyone's views, not just those who 'shout the loudest'?

✓ how will you finish the event in a positive way?

✓ can you provide feedback on the results of the event, to show it was worthwhile taking part?

Engaging with large numbers of residents

Many pathfinders have carried out surveys of attitudes towards the problems which the pathfinder intends to tackle, and the results have been used to guide objectives and priorities. BNG is a particularly lively example.

BNG's consultation 'What makes a great place to live?'

BNG used consultants Urbanistix to run roadshow events and collect resident opinion across the pathfinder area. They used techniques such as a short film, a puppet show and story boards to attract people and inform them about the pathfinder prior to getting their views. People were able to write their views onto 'picture boards'. People were also able to complete written surveys via numerous formats such as post, email and an interactive website. During the six-week period over 400 people were engaged in the four roadshow events and about 740 written responses were received.

Results suggested agreement with the pathfinder's focus on increasing home ownership, greater housing choice and better neighbourhoods. The findings of the consultation enabled BNG to refine its vision and objectives and helped the pathfinder when it put together its scheme update.

Source: Urbanistix (2005) *Community and Stakeholder Communication and Consultation Results for BNG Scheme Update.*

A limitation of wide-scale surveys is that they are only likely to give a very broad guide to people's views, and may in the end produce rather obvious findings or ones which (because opinions expressed have to be digested and presented by those writing up the surveys) summarise a lot of different views in a bland way. Also, spontaneously-given opinions (as with market research) may be useful in terms of attitudes towards specific things (like a new product in the shops) but less so in relation to wider concepts, that need explanation and discussion, like market renewal. Careful attention needs to be given in survey design to posing questions which generate responses and provide material which is readily analysable and gives meaningful results.

Another disadvantage of wide-scale surveys is the potential exclusion of 'hard-to-reach' groups. Most pathfinders have dealt with this by 'outreach' work — arranging meetings (perhaps through intermediaries, such as voluntary organisations) with people such as BME women's groups, older people (who may not go to evening meetings), children and young people. UL carried out specific needs research with refugees and asylum seekers because of their significance in the local population and in the future of the area.

UL research on housing needs of refugees and asylum seekers

Urban Living commissioned research on the employment prospects and housing needs of asylum seekers and refugees living in north west Birmingham, allowing the link between potential income levels and housing choices to be considered. The research gave a valuable insight into the likely future of this part of the market, looking at the difference between the requirements and behaviour of asylum seekers and refugees.

The pathfinder has used the research findings to develop its action plan for the private rented sector, to commission new research and to inform the development of various strategies and programmes. Urban Living will evaluate which approaches to supported housing are most successful in helping refugees to become self-sufficient in the longer term.

Urban Living supported Family HA's bid for hact funding to establish a pilot Refugee Housing Partnership for north west Birmingham, which produced a joint action plan for improving housing services across all sectors for refugees. It also provided training for frontline staff in local housing associations.

As at August 2006, around 2,800 accession state migrants had been recorded as coming to live within the pathfinder boundary. Urban Living has taken the lead among the pathfinders in accessing and analysing data from the Home Office. Urban Living has used the results of focus groups with refugees and EU migrants to inform its scheme update, strategies and interventions.

Source: Audit Commission (2005) *Housing Market Renewal*, p31 and information from UL.

3. What standards about community engagement should be set at strategic level?

An example of principles set for community engagement applying across a pathfinder area is provided by BNG.

BNG community engagement strategy

BNG set the following principles for community engagement:

- to be inclusive – providing opportunities for all groups to be engaged
- make sure people know about the opportunities to be involved, and support that involvement by removing barriers

→

- be honest about what we are involving people in and what can be achieved
- be timely – involve people and make sure people have enough time to be effectively engaged
- consider what people have already been asked and what they have said
- evaluate responses and demonstrate how they had the opportunity to influence the decision
- provide feedback to everyone affected.

The community engagement strategy is set to be revised following the recent community engagement evaluation.

Source: Bridging NewcastleGateshead (undated) *Community Engagement Strategy*.

For this guide, a set of CIH/TPAS Recommended Standards has been prepared (see annex) which aims to include all relevant aspects of community engagement covered in the guide and set out standards for HMR pathfinders which other agencies can modify and adopt locally in their regeneration programmes. The standards also take into account, and are partially based on, the Audit Commission's KLOE (key lines of enquiry) on resident involvement in housing.

Given the nature of the HMR programme, with strategies being set at pathfinder level that are then delivered by different local partners, it is crucial not only to have overall policies on engagement but also ways of ensuring they are carried out, monitored and adapted as the work proceeds. Having an engagement strategy is not just a paper exercise and community engagement cannot be seen as a stage to 'get through' but is embedded in the work of the pathfinder and its partners.

[Standards 1.2, 1.3]

4. How can communications aimed at residents be made readily understandable?

Communications aimed at residents sometimes have unrealistic 'architect's impressions', difficult-to-read plans, or simply too much detailed text. Below is a checklist against which communications with residents might be reviewed before they are finalised. (Ideas for tackling this issue at neighbourhood level are given in chapter 5).

[Standard 2.1]

Overall checklist for communications aimed at residents

✓ what is the audience? has the material been prepared with them in mind?

✓ what format is being used? if in print – is this the best method? should it be complemented by others (eg face-to-face discussion?)

✓ have you checked it for plain English? (for example, have you given it to some residents to read, or perhaps non-technical staff in the team?)

✓ where jargon or acronyms have to be used, are they explained?

✓ is it succinct and to the point? can it be read and digested in five minutes?

✓ does it readily gain someone's attention?

✓ but have you also checked that any graphics or illustrations look realistic?

✓ have you avoided futuristic drawings? – are any presentations of proposals as accurate as possible, enabling ordinary people to visualise them easily? have you tested this out?

✓ what measures will you take to make sure you get the information across to everyone? – have you considered alternative languages and measures for communicating with hard-to-reach groups?

✓ are you relying only on one form of communication? can you back it up by others (one-to-one visits, street meetings, etc)?

✓ what result do you want? if it is to obtain views, is it clear to people how they can respond?

---

5. How should priorities for engagement be established at strategic level?

It is unlikely that agencies will be able to carry out activities in every neighbourhood at the same time, or with the same commitment of resources. Decisions have already been made by all the pathfinders to prioritise certain areas, both in terms of the stage at which they are tackled in the work programme and the degree of intervention envisaged.

While these decisions need to be kept under review as circumstances change or new information comes to light, partners need to be clear about the priorities and the implications, and be prepared to explain this to residents. In areas where intensive action (eg redevelopment) is taking place, there may be adjoining areas where residents are also keen for intervention to take place but may have to be told that works are planned for a later stage in the renewal process.

[Standard 2.2]

6. How can consistency be achieved – in messages from the lead agency and its partners, and in treatment of different parts of the area?

Local authorities have their own representation mechanisms, programmes and statutory responsibilities, and social sector landlords (LAs and HAs) have specific responsibilities to involve tenants. Inevitably there will be a sharing of responsibilities between the partner agencies, and the degree of sharing depends on a range of factors including the current and past history of engagement and the experience held by the different bodies. There needs to be a degree of pragmatism and realism about sharing arrangements. For example, one agency in an area may have staff experienced in engagement work and have mechanisms 'up and running', while another does not.

In deciding or reviewing the split of responsibilities, the sort of questions that should be asked are set out in the checklist below. More detail on auditing staff skills in community engagement is given in chapter 8.

Checklist for sharing responsibilities between agencies

✓ what experience is there of community engagement and who has it?

✓ what knowledge is there of key communities or constituencies (eg ethnic minorities) within the regeneration area?

✓ are there staff with direct experience through their work, where they live, etc? – are they in the lead agency itself or in the LA or an HA?

✓ what gaps exist?

✓ are there current neighbourhood-level initiatives which will continue and for which engagement mechanisms already exist?

✓ how can the regeneration programme support or build on these?

✓ who has current responsibility for and knowledge about the range of existing community organisations (eg residents' and tenants' bodies)?

✓ what measures are needed to get LA or HA frontline staff 'on board' with what the agency is doing and avoid negative or conflicting messages?

✓ what ongoing mechanisms are needed to ensure consistency of approach across the regeneration area, among any different agencies working at local level?

✓ is the sharing of responsibilities for engagement consistent with the division of responsibilities on other issues, eg finance, and programme delivery?

Of key importance are the history of and skills available for community engagement. Residents will want to see how current arrangements fit logically with previous engagement mechanisms. Furthermore, skills in engaging with residents, and knowledge about the communities involved, are both scarce resources. A crucial element must be the sharing of history, skills and knowledge to best effect in securing the ongoing engagement of residents in the programme.

In the HMR programme, mechanisms for ensuring consistency of approach across the pathfinder include:

- A community engagement working group – BNG has a 'workstream' on engagement which draws from the pathfinder, the two LAs, the delivery agencies and residents' groups, meeting bi-monthly.
- A common budget for community engagement – eg in BNG and MSP.
- Regular briefings for local authority councillors – eg as in RNS – to ensure they are well-informed and if possible 'on board' with the programme.
- Approved panels for consultants, developers, etc, enabling the pathfinder to get agencies to 'sign up to' principles about engagement – as in RNS.

Where the pathfinder is reliant on statutory processes being carried out by the local authority – such as Neighbourhood Renewal Assessments (using housing legislation) or Local Development Frameworks (planning) – it is vital that the parameters are agreed in advance, and that proposals developed for different parts of the pathfinder area are compatible with each other. (There is at least one example where so much new development was proposed in different neighbourhoods that in total it posed an unrealistic target for the pathfinder to achieve.)

Particular issues arise in using consultants because of the usually time-limited nature of their work. These are dealt with in chapter 9.

[Standard 1.2]

7. What ways are there of recognising community initiatives, and of building capacity within communities?

Chapter 3 suggested that developing residents' confidence and capacities is a key aim of community engagement. It is important enough to warrant recognition at strategic level, in the mechanisms created and the resources deployed. It is also an issue that needs consideration as part of the detailed work in each neighbourhood. For the HMR pathfinders, we consider three possible tasks – building ownership of ideas and plans, stimulating community initiatives, and building community capacity.

Building ownership of ideas and plans
One issue that is particularly challenging is deciding to what extent residents' views should be sought and taken on board before any action is taken, as against the desire to gain early 'wins' to move the programme forward as quickly as possible and to convince people that 'things are happening'.

This issue can only be decided locally by people in tune with community feelings. For example, Gateway have put a premium on putting finalised proposals on the table and achieving early action, whereas RNS have deliberately paced things more slowly so that people understand and approve each step in the process. Both approaches are logical given their different histories. Whichever is followed, the principle of building ownership of ideas at the local level is very important. Normally this is most readily done by having a 'blank sheet of paper' and building up ideas *with* residents. However, the paper can rarely be completely 'blank' and prompt action on some things may preclude detailed consultation. Residents understand practicalities and that some things may be 'non-negotiable' – the important thing is to build their trust and maximise the areas where they can have a decisive influence on what happens.

This debate is needed at strategic level, so that all partners own the principles that are to be followed.

Ways of building ownership of ideas and plans include:
- techniques such as 'Planning for Real' or 'Enquiry by Design' (see chapter 6)
- visits or interchanges with other areas or regeneration schemes (UL have taken local Bangladeshi residents on visits to shared ownership schemes in other areas, to develop familiarisation with how they work and whether residents like them)
- implementation groups dealing with particular projects (eg in Sheffield, see chapter 6)
- full-blown involvement in design, and implementation of the result (see examples in chapter 6).

Stimulating community initiatives
Sustainable communities are ones in which (among other things) people take initiatives of their own to improve the neighbourhood, put forward proposals to the local council, or tackle problems like anti-social behaviour. Agencies will want to stimulate initiatives of these kinds – both those related directly to the programme and in more general ways. This may include the following:
- creating a 'community initiatives fund' as part of the community engagement budget, to which groups can apply
- competitions (such as BNG's 'Dream Bedroom' competition for schoolchildren)
- making use of local voluntary organisations wherever possible
- initiatives such as 'Living through Change' in Sefton (NH), which provides funding for measures to improve the local environment – see chapter 6
- ensuring that resident initiatives are rewarded – for example, the residents' association in Fiveways, Rock Ferry, won one of the Merseyside 'Strictly Regeneration' awards for their engagement in regeneration of their area.

Building community capacity

Community capacity-building is 'activities, resources and support that strengthen the skills, abilities and confidence of people and community groups to take effective action and leading roles in the development of their communities'.[9] There is considerable guidance on this subject, and there are government programmes such as ChangeUp to provide resources for capacity building. More detail is given on this topic in chapter 12.

[Standard 7.1]

8. How does the lead agency judge the overall effectiveness of community engagement?

It is important that the commitment to community engagement includes a process for evaluating whether it is successful or not, and (see below) for learning from it.

Informal evaluation is likely to include:

- feedback from residents at one-to-one advice sessions, neighbourhood meetings, etc
- feedback through local representatives, such as councillors (perhaps in the briefing sessions mentioned earlier), community-based workers, etc
- letters to the press, calls to local radio, etc.

More formal evaluation might include:

- monitoring attendance levels at meetings, advice surgeries, etc
- using 'feedback forms' or other forms of monitoring at meetings, exhibitions, show houses and similar occasions
- having a complaints system and monitoring the results.

BNG decided to commission consultants to evaluate the effectiveness of its community engagement measures (see below).

Consultants assess effectiveness of community engagement activity within BNG area

BNG appointed consultants QA Research to measure the effectiveness of community engagement and identify gaps. QA looked at issues such as whether engagement is reaching all parts of the community, how it relates to other community engagement processes in the same areas, any barriers to communication, the effectiveness of BNG's branding, etc.

→

---

9   Definition in Home Office (2004) *Firm Foundations*.

QA provided guidance and identified good practice. BNG did not specify the research methods to be used but invited consultants to put forward proposals as part of their bids.

The evaluation was completed in September 2006 and a community engagement workshop held in December 2006 to consider findings. Based on the outcomes of this workshop, the existing community engagement strategy will be refined.

More information: Contact Michelle Playford 0191 277 2665 or michelle.playford@bridgingng.org.uk

The lead agency can establish procedures to be applied to community engagement, to ensure that each activity (public meeting, focus group, etc) can be evaluated after the event.

Checklist for evaluating community engagement activities

✓ what do you plan to achieve by the exercise (survey, meeting, etc) you are carrying out?

✓ have you set some measurable targets (eg numbers of people attending) and some mechanism for recording what happens?

✓ will you be able to assess whether there is balanced representation, or whether you have only reached certain groups? what will you do to follow this up?

✓ is it appropriate to have a mechanism for getting people's comments such as feedback forms, storyboards, etc? have you put these in place?

✓ are you keeping a record of what people say? to whom will it be reported, and in what form?

✓ what follow-up are you planning? have you arranged to tell people what the outcome of their comments was?

✓ does someone have clear responsibility for taking forward the views expressed to ensure that the activity has a successful outcome?

✓ what can we learn for the next exercise of this kind, or in the same community?

[Standard 6.1]

9. How does the lead agency learn from community engagement, linking it to what went before and what will follow the regeneration programme?

Finally, community engagement does not take place in a vacuum. There are several ways in which the HMR pathfinders' work illustrates this:

A prior history of engagement?

In many cases the communities will have been 'consulted' on proposals before. There may even be a track record of issues or problems which will affect the pathfinder's work and of which it should try to be aware. Part of the understanding of the neighbourhoods in which the pathfinder is working must include its past history of engagement with the local authority, with previous regeneration schemes, and with other agencies.

Other processes that overlap with the pathfinder?

In several cases pathfinders have 'inherited' ongoing regeneration programmes where engagement is already happening. Or there may be parallel but related exercises such as a stock transfer, development of an ALMO, etc, which involve consultation. Pathfinders will want to make sure they are aware of and take account of these. Where regeneration or redevelopment projects have been subsumed into the pathfinder, are they now being run to the same standards of engagement as the pathfinder applies to its own activities?

And for the future?

Part of the learning process represented by the pathfinder programme is to set practices in place that will be continued by local authorities and other agencies. Another aspect of learning is to ensure that what the community says is recorded and passed on to those agencies.

[Standard 7.2]

CHAPTER 5

ENGAGING AT NEIGHBOURHOOD LEVEL – GETTING STARTED

What this chapter is about

- the ground rules for community engagement
- defining neighbourhoods and deciding timescales
- establishing the context for the work
- understanding the neighbourhood

What are the 'ground rules' for engaging the community?

Clearly it is work at the level of the individual neighbourhood that is the essence of community engagement in housing-led regeneration. This chapter deals with the preparatory stages of engagement at this level, and chapter 6 with the development and implementation of detailed proposals.

Deciding who takes the lead role in community engagement – the strategic agency, the LA or a local housing association – was considered in chapter 4. Whoever takes the lead (in this and the next chapter called 'the team') will need to decide the scope of engagement in the particular neighbourhood, against the background of the wider strategy and the available resources.

Inevitably, a balance must be struck. On the one hand, residents are not likely to be offered a completely 'blank sheet' because the team is constrained as to what it *can* do, and the team will make an assessment of the issues and some ideas about what it *will do* in the area as a result of the surveys and other work it carries out. On the other hand, it must not give the impression – nor should it be the case – that it already has 'a plan' for the area: there must be a good deal of genuine scope for people to put forward ideas. The team needs to know what any boundaries are.

Among the issues that may need to be decided at the outset are:

- How is the neighbourhood to be defined (see below)?
- What are the goals and timescale of the engagement process?
- How will the team respond to the kinds of issues and ideas likely to emerge?
- Who is 'in charge' at neighbourhood level? How much flexibility have they got? To what extent can the community itself be 'in charge' of the process?
- Are the different agencies that will determine the future of the area committed to the timetable? Will they commit time to it and respond properly to issues and proposals that arise?
- How will the results from engagement be fed back into strategic decisions by the local authority and other agencies? Will this be done in a transparent way?
- Is there a commitment to feed back to the community the results of their ideas and proposals?
- What resources are available for the process itself (see checklist)? Does whoever is in charge have command of the resources (eg to buy in consultancy time) that they might need?

Checklist for a neighbourhood-level engagement budget

Does it need to include:

✓ consultancy costs?

✓ costs of surveys?

✓ publicity costs – leaflets, newsletters, exhibitions?

✓ costs of meetings – room hire, costs of a facilitator/interpreter?

✓ costs of a local presence – drop-in facilities or a local office?

✓ resources for training and/or community capacity building?

✓ allowances for running costs for eg a new residents' association?

[Standards 2.3 and 5.1]

How big a neighbourhood?

This is not an issue on which the guide need spend much time, since what matters is what agencies consider to be 'neighbourhoods' in their particular area. Government policy has tended to focus on areas of around 4-5,000 households, or 10,000 people.

In practice this is likely to be the upper limit of neighbourhood size for detailed planning and engagement work. The CIH guide to neighbourhood management,[10] which looks at this issue in more detail, suggests a pragmatic approach to defining neighbourhood boundaries, based on the views of people living there. In some pathfinders (for example, Wirral, NH – see page 56) residents found it difficult to engage at a large scale and engagement was more successful when 'neighbourhoods' were broken down into smaller areas to which people more readily relate.

On the other hand, it is also a common experience that people accept that a neighbourhood should change, but they may be reluctant to accept the consequences at the level of their own street or house. While this cannot be avoided (and may be successfully tackled), it does mean that the neighbourhood has to be sufficiently big that initial engagement can be about issues that affect everyone, not just the future of small groups of properties.

Which community?

Defining a 'community' is even more difficult. This guide does not attempt a definition but uses the term in a general sense to mean the people living in a neighbourhood.

Two points need to be made. One is that (of course) any community is multi-faceted – it might be better to think of several different communities sharing an area, rather than there being 'a community'.[11] And attempts at engagement need to 'reach out' to groups within the community that might not readily 'engage' through public meetings, surveys, or other conventional approaches. The guide returns to this point in chapter 6.

Another issue relates to measures of success in engaging with a community. Even vigorous and varied methods of engagement, intended to appeal to all the different groups within a community, will in most cases only be partially successful. Detailed engagement in small areas, where people are consulted on a crucial issue (eg demolition), can on the other hand produce near 100% coverage (eg the Reema Estate in Thurnscoe, TSY – see page 66). But expectations about the likely 'success rate' in larger areas need to be tempered accordingly.

What timescales are being followed?

In all of the pathfinder areas, questions about the timing and timescales of engagement at neighbourhood level have needed consideration. At what stage should engagement start in a particular area? Over what time period should engagement last? How does

10 Duncan, P and Thomas, S (2007) *Successful Neighbourhoods: A good practice guide*. CIH.
11 See Taylor, M (1992) *Signposts to Community Development*. Community Development Foundation. A short guide to communities and to 'community development'.

this relate to the date on which physical change might begin? And over what timescale for the future of the neighbourhood is any 'vision' or plan for it to be prepared?

These are issues on which it is impossible to be prescriptive – in some areas there may be problems needing immediate attention, and on which a consensus can be rapidly achieved. In others there may be intractable problems (such as buying out incompatible industrial uses) which may take several years to resolve, and where there is necessarily more opportunity to consider a variety of options on how to use the land made available.

All of the pathfinders have, though, prioritised engagement between one neighbourhood and another in some way, reflecting the seriousness and urgency of poor housing conditions, and/or the extent of housing market weakness. For example, RNS's initial focus has been on four 'Areas of Major Intervention', to be followed by a number of 'General Renewal Areas' where action is less urgent.

When it is their neighbourhood's 'turn', experience suggests that residents want action taken on priority issues, where consensus can be achieved, in a relatively short time – no longer than 1-2 years. In several areas of Hull, for example, residents are pushing for demolition to take place quickly and want no further delays.

Residents may be happy to deliberate on more challenging issues, such as types of new housing development, over a longer time frame and looking rather further ahead – say up to 5-10 years, providing early action is being taken on some key issues.

Experience in Wirral (NH) is probably typical in that people have difficulty in identifying with – or seeing as realistic – plans for longer periods of 10-15 years or more. If these are sometimes needed, it is important to show the 'stepping stones' in the process leading to the longer-term vision, and what changes this will produce in the shorter term. It is important to emphasise as well – but also to be careful about – the fact that the plans for the area are aimed at future residents as well as present ones (perhaps by indicating that young people's aspirations have to be considered alongside those of older residents).

Experience also suggests that flexibility is required in setting targets for decision-making on crucial issues, especially (see below) if there is a past history of engagement with a neighbourhood that has created mistrust or other obstacles. For example, in Sheffield, engagement in the masterplanning in one area was programmed to last six months but eventually took 18. However, the outcome was judged to be a success because of the level of engagement achieved and the fact that the proposals changed significantly as a result.

[Standard 2.2]

Is there a 'past history' of engagement?

Even adjacent neighbourhoods can vary considerably in this respect. Some have an extensive past history of previous community engagement and regeneration initiatives, which may or may not have been successful. In Newcastle, the West End area has been subject to at least eight major regeneration programmes, starting in the 1970s.[12] It would be surprising if this had not produced a degree of 'consultation fatigue'. This can be reduced or avoided by, as far as possible, not 'going over old ground' in new consultations. However, maintaining the momentum of engagement in an area is always a challenge.

In Thurnscoe (TSY) and in parts of the RNS pathfinder, residents had had little prior contact with local authorities. The task was to build trust and show that the pathfinder and its partners are fully engaged with the needs of the neighbourhoods and are committed to talking to residents and taking their views on board.

In any area, it is important to have an 'audit' of prior community engagement and regeneration exercises, which shows what was carried out, how it was done and who by – and if possible the successes and failures in engaging with the community and any lessons that were learnt. Such an audit was carried out by, for example, Blackburn (EEL).

[Standard 2.4]

Is there a context for preparing masterplans?

Planning for change in a particular neighbourhood can only take place satisfactorily in the context of a strategy for the wider urban area in which the neighbourhood sits. This may already exist, or may have to be developed as part of the pathfinder's work. An illustration of how neighbourhood planning fits within a hierarchy of decision-making about an area is provided by Thurnscoe (TSY):

- *An Overall Strategy for the Barnsley Housing Market Renewal Area* was developed by consultants EDAW, covering all of the towns and villages included in the HMR area.
- *Thurnscoe Village profile* (see page 48) looks at the future of the whole Thurnscoe village, within the parameters of the overall strategy.
- *East Thurnscoe* was the subject of a detailed action plan (see page 55).
- *Individual house visits* determined the approach in the area where demolition and new housing was proposed.

---

12 See Robinson, F (2005) *Regenerating the West End of Newcastle: What went wrong?* (available from www.sustainable-cities.org.uk/Database_files).

Chapter 11 deals with the issue of avoiding duplication of consultation and ensuring that requirements for statutory planning processes are dealt with at the same time as regeneration-led masterplanning.

Understanding the neighbourhood

Basic information about each neighbourhood includes: who lives there, how this is changing, how the area is viewed, what the issues are, what community organisations or representative groups already exist. (The range of information needed is set out in detail in the *Neighbourhood Renewal Assessment Guidance Manual*.)[13] There is no single way of getting this information – any neighbourhood is likely to require several 'ways in' to developing an understanding of it. These will range from the formal to the highly informal – chatting to people, going along to existing activities in the area such as mother and toddler groups, using local shops, and so on.

This is also a continuous process, in which the team will start with limited knowledge and build it up over time. This puts a premium on consistency in engaging with people in the neighbourhood, having a team with at least some staff dedicated to working in that area long-term, if possible with a local presence (or least some kind of 'surgery' or 'drop-in' arrangements), and able to build up both the formal and informal knowledge of how the area works.

Here is a list of possible approaches to developing an understanding of particular neighbourhoods, largely drawn from the pathfinders (with examples where appropriate) or from work in similar areas.

Neighbourhood audits

An audit of available information about an area – its past history (see above), present contacts (eg with the council), residents' organisations and other community groups, community facilities (eg meeting places, community development workers, local projects, advice centres), any local media (eg neighbourhood newspapers), formal bodies such as faith groups, programmes operating in the area (eg Sure Start), information on the make-up of the community (ethnicity, age breakdown, turnover, etc). The aim is not to collect reams of information but to build a picture of what is already happening and what points of engagement with the community might already exist. In the process of doing this and starting to talk to people, the team will inevitably start to get impressions about the problems and issues in the area.

---

13 ODPM (2004), section 7 (http://www.neighbourhood.gov.uk/publications.asp?did=1540).

Community walkabouts

A group of official-looking people walking around an area and looking at buildings will inevitably attract attention and comment. By doing this with known community leaders, or perhaps ward councillors, local people can be drawn into discussions and problems identified – especially those that are visible that the group can be taken to see. Middlesbrough, a non-pathfinder area, conducted two days of such walkabouts, involving about 40 residents, producing profiles of the neighbourhood and information (such as digital photographs) used in later engagement.

Neighbourhood profiles or surveys

This refers to actual door-to-door surveys, intended both to find out about the characteristics of people living in a neighbourhood and get their views on the issues it faces and the priorities between them.

Thurnscoe Village Profile

In Thurnscoe (TSY), Barnsley Council produced a 16-page 'village profile' from survey work carried out by its own staff. The profile distinguished between the views of older and younger residents, and gave an immediate 'picture' of the area's problems, including some first ideas of how to tackle them.

Stakeholder interviews

Middlesbrough carried out 'stakeholder interviews' with key people in the neighbourhood – ward councillors, faith leaders, community representatives, key business people, community workers, etc. These had the same aim of building up information about the area and its problems, but also served to make contact with and explain the intentions of the regeneration programme.

Assembling and sharing data on the area

All lead agencies need to collect data about the characteristics of neighbourhoods, house condition, population turnover, house prices, and so on as part of their evidence base. If this can be maintained, updated and presented in a dynamic way, not only does this help inform technical work (eg design and masterplanning) but can also capture people's interest.

Tracking neighbourhood change in Manchester/Salford

Both councils are using a Geographic Information System (GIS) based tool to track a number of indicators in HMR areas. These include a range of housing statistics such as house prices, turnover, voids and tenure change, but also pointers to the 'health' of the neighbourhood such as those relating to employment, educational attainment, crime and anti-social behaviour, health, etc.

The indicators can be utilised at very localised area level, and can be checked at different points in time, enabling (for example) a picture of progress to be obtained before, during and after a major intervention in a neighbourhood, such as redevelopment, housing, streetscape and environmental improvements, etc – and can allow for the evaluation of the impact of HMR and related investment (education, neighbourhood management, etc.) over the medium and long term.

More information: Rebecca Chambers, Manchester Salford Pathfinder
r.chambers@manchester.gov.uk

Data such as that generated by GIS can be a powerful tool, but of course is only as good as the information being put into it. It is important to consider how to share the use of such systems with residents, build their capacity to understand them and enable them to challenge or debate the results.

[Standard 1.5]

CHAPTER 6

ENGAGING AT NEIGHBOURHOOD LEVEL – DEVELOPING AND IMPLEMENTING DETAILED PLANS

What this chapter is about

- getting started
- generating ideas
- barriers to engagement
- engaging with hard-to-reach groups

- keeping people informed
- specific issues that arise
- final proposals for the neighbourhood
- learning and feedback

Starting to engage with the community

Developing understanding about a neighbourhood, which was considered in chapter 5, is bound to mean engaging with people in it to some extent. But this is likely to be swiftly followed by the start of the engagement process itself, when the team in the area announces its presence and begins to talk to people in detail.

Some of the methods that might be used to kickstart the process are these:

Contacting key people in the area

From the work done to find out about the neighbourhood (chapter 5), it should be apparent who the key people are in the area – faith leaders, shopkeepers, people running advice centres, etc. Before holding events such as a residents' meeting to launch the work in the area, it is worth contacting them and explaining what is happening and what the team aims to do – and seek their advice or suggestions. This helps to avoid having the same people say that 'it's the first I've heard about it' when the meeting or event occurs.

An 'event'

In the Walker district of Newcastle, engagement in an area is always started by an 'event' of some kind to draw people's attention to what is happening. One of these was a *community inquiry* into what was wrong with and what was needed in the area. Some sort of follow-up is obviously required, such as setting up groups of residents who will continue to be involved in detailed planning for the area. In Thurnscoe (TSY), an *exhibition* was held which fed back to residents the issues that arose in the initial survey and put forward possible solutions. Holding the exhibition over a few days made it possible for residents to see it, talk to neighbours about it, then return to record their views.

Joining in with established events or groups

Another approach is for staff to ask to attend established meetings in an area – at the mosque, a mother and toddler group, etc. The advantage of doing so is that people are likely to be there for everyday reasons and it may therefore be less confrontational than holding a public meeting.

Contacting or establishing residents' associations

RNS has a practice of finding out if active residents' groups already exist in an area, and attempting to engage with them on an ongoing basis. If there are none, staff invite residents to form one to provide a point of regular contact as plans develop.

Public meetings

There are very mixed views on the value of public meetings, and whether they are a good idea is likely to vary a lot from area to area, depending on its character, history and local personalities. On the one hand such meetings can be dominated and exploited by a few vociferous individuals (or even taken over by political or hostile groups). On the other they do represent an 'event' which people will remember, and can (if they go well) be a way of building consensus or establishing residents' committees or working groups. Below is some advice on the 'basics' of holding public meetings – see the box on the next page.

In Sandwell (UL) a public meeting was followed by smaller group sessions with interpreters for different languages, and this format worked well.

Agreeing on the issues that need to be tackled

Obviously, in starting to engage with the community, there must be something to engage about. The *Neighbourhood Renewal Assessment Guidance Manual* gives an example (see box on the next page) of the kind of issues, questions and possible answers that might be agreed, based on the appraisal of the neighbourhood discussed in chapter 5.

Public meetings – do's and don'ts

Do	Don't
✓ ensure there is adequate notice of time and place	✗ choose a location that is difficult for (say) older people to get to
✓ have experienced and senior staff available to answer questions	✗ go unprepared to the meeting, eg without up-to-date knowledge of local concerns
✓ get all the relevant agencies along	✗ have a confrontational room layout, eg a raised platform
✓ make sure interpreter facilities are there, if needed	✗ have lengthy, complicated presentations
✓ consider having an independent chair	✗ take major decisions (eg about demolition) unless people knew this was to happen and/or there are others ways in which people can make their views known
✓ consider breaking up into smaller groups so everyone can have their say	✗ allow a few people to dominate proceedings

Bowtown workshop discussion

Where are we now? (the area as it currently is)
The area has traditionally been a low cost area and the housing a bit run down but it is in a good location close to town. The area has been declining; the community is changing and is now no longer a decent place to live. Crime is rising, there is a lot of unemployment and in some parts houses are not selling.

How did we get here? (if the area has declined why is this?)
The area has not had the level of investment that some other parts of the borough have enjoyed and people cannot afford to improve their houses themselves. The main reason why it is no longer a decent place to live is because the community has become less stable and crime is perceived as a major concern.

Where are we going if current trends persist? (if there is no intervention in the area)
No new people will want to buy in the area and the pockets of abandonment will get worse until there are only private renters and those without the resources to move left.

Where do we want to be?
A viable, sustainable community where people choose to live. Everyone has access to decent housing, enabled by improvements to existing housing, removal of redundant stock and provision of new houses for larger families.

Source: *Neighbourhood Renewal Assessment Guidance Manual*, section 6.

Methods for generating options for change

The *Neighbourhood Renewal Assessment Guidance Manual* describes in detail the option generation process, but from a technical viewpoint. (In this chapter it is assumed that procedures similar to those in the manual are being followed, and the dimension covered here is engaging with communities as part of the process.)

Some pathfinders have begun engagement with as open a process as possible, designed to get people involved, working together and generating ideas. Here are some examples of different approaches to planning with a 'blank sheet'.

Community planning weekends

An elaborate but highly effective way of generating momentum for change and getting all parties involved in producing a plan of action for a site or neighbourhood.

Community planning weekends comprise an intensive and carefully structured programme of activities spanning a weekend or perhaps Friday to Monday. The main workshop sessions are open to the general public. The weekends are facilitated by a multidisciplinary team. This may be comprised of outsiders or locals or a combination of the two.

The end result is a set of proposals for action which is presented to the community on the last day and perhaps produced in exhibition and print form.

A similar method, 'Enquiry by Design', was used in Nelson (see example below).

'Planning for Real'

'Planning for Real' uses simple models as a focus for people to put forward and prioritise ideas on how their area can be improved. It is a highly visible, hands-on community development and empowerment tool, which people of all abilities and backgrounds find easy and enjoyable to engage in.

A large 3-dimensional model of a neighbourhood is constructed, preferably by local people, using cardboard cut-outs for buildings pasted onto a base plan fixed to polystyrene or cardboard. The model is used at pre-advertised sessions held in various locations in the community.

Participants place suggestion cards on the model indicating what they want to see happen and where (eg new houses, playground, parking, trees, shops). The cards are sorted and prioritised to establish an action plan which is followed up by working groups.

One disadvantage mentioned in one pathfinder area was that 'Planning for Real' is too open-ended, and it is difficult to take account of the real constraints on action that always exist.

Design games

Design games are like jigsaw puzzles. They are a highly visual way of allowing people to explore physical design options for a site or internal space. They are particularly useful for designing parks and room layouts and can also be used for land-use planning. They can be used in isolation or as part of a broader participation process.

A base map of a site or room is prepared. Cut-out pieces representing items that could be incorporated are made to the same scale. Materials for making pieces are kept at hand to allow new items to be made as desired. Individuals or groups move pieces around until they are happy with the design, which is then photographed.

Ideas competitions

Ideas competitions are a good way of stimulating creative thinking and generating interest and momentum. They can be designed to allow everyone a chance to put forward their ideas or be just for professionals.

Ideas competitions are normally held at the start of the development process or when there is opposition to a proposed scheme. They can be simple and immediate or highly complex. A brief is produced, clearly setting out the task, entry format and deadline, judging procedure, eligibility and relevant background. The task can be to produce general ideas for improving an area or proposals for a specific site, building or problem.

Judging can done by a panel or through using a public voting system. Alternatively different organisations can make separate awards. Winning entries are widely publicised and published to secure momentum for implementation.

[Above examples are based on: http://www.communityplanning.net/methods/methods.htm – this website has a much longer list of possible methods. BNG's *Community Engagement Strategy* also has an extensive, similar list.]

Approaches in practice

No approach to work in a neighbourhood is quite the same as another – all have to be adapted to local circumstances. Here are six examples of approaches to developing options for neighbourhoods, from six different pathfinders.

Meir, Stoke-on-Trent (RNS)

Planning for the regeneration of Meir began in 2004. Engagement is led by a local steering group, chaired by a resident, which includes residents, councillors and local business people. They worked with community architects PTE (who were appointed by the residents) to develop a masterplan over a period of 6-9 months, involving more than 60 local meetings, including sub-group sessions with young people, older people and BME people. A range of proposals includes demolishing 460 houses and building 415 new ones, as well as wider improvements in the area. After the masterplan received local support, the proposals are being included in a statutory plan prepared by the city council. Surveys of individual families' housing needs will influence the detail of the new development.

East Thurnscoe, Barnsley (TSY)

The East Thurnscoe Estate of approximately 1000 properties was included in the Thurnscoe Village Survey (see chapter 5), and was then identified for more detailed masterplanning because of its range of problems. The masterplanning identified various key issues, such as empty properties, poor quality boundaries, absentee landlords, anti-social behaviour, inappropriate housing types and poor quality open space. Feedback from consultations highlighted a particular area within the estate known more commonly as the 'bull ring'. A number of 'community planning days' were held to identify the issues in this area in more detail and generate options. Technical staff fed back to residents on the feasibility of the options and any potential problems, which led for example to sheltered housing being preferred over a public garden.

Eventually a plan has emerged which involves some demolition, new build, improved open spaces and extensive environmental improvements. The details of demolition were actually decided by one-to-one visits to establish who wanted to be rehoused, and this is now in progress.

Bensham, Gateshead (BNG)

This large neighbourhood (8,000 properties, mainly 'Tyneside flats') with a range of different problems now has an area action plan after a year of community engagement. This began in January, 2005 with a survey and community audit, followed by 'walkabouts' with community representatives. By April the process led to outline ideas for the area, and then in June to more detailed options including some demolition.

→

By September a draft plan was ready, which included demolition but at a lower scale than envisaged at the earlier stage. About 400 houses will be cleared, and largely replaced with affordable family houses for sale. Overall, there is about 80% community support for the proposals, but a local residents' group still actively opposes demolition and meetings with them have not changed their views.

More information: Contact Craig Ellis on 0191 433 3229 or email craigellis@gateshead.gov.uk

Fiveways, Rock Ferry (NH)

Wirral MBC changed its approach to masterplanning, from using consultants to produce long-range plans for large areas, to one in which much smaller areas receive more detailed attention. This is particularly important where demolition is involved.

In Fiveways, planning for the future of this very mixed-tenure estate began with identification of and agreement about the problems – anti-social behaviour, poorly-managed privately-rented housing, poor environment, etc. Owner-occupiers led the planning process and a range of options were considered. Initially the residents wanted the whole area to be redeveloped but some demolition of houses and buying-out of former industrial sites will enable densities to be reduced.

More information: Nicola Rigby on 0151 691 8249 / 07957 640456

Toxteth Street, East Manchester (MSP)

Engagement here began at the end of 2001 with a series of 'drop-in' sessions, which led to a steering group of residents and local voluntary bodies being set up, early in 2002. This set out key principles that would be followed in a neighbour-hood plan, such as achieving better management of the area, creating a better housing mix, improving the existing housing, etc. During the rest of 2002 residents' views were obtained (using consultants Optima Housing) by a variety of methods such as surveys, a roadshow, drop-ins and study tours. This led to a report on which detailed proposals could be based.

In April 2003 a developer (Lovell) and architect (PTE) were chosen, who produced a 'vision' for the area which was the subject of further consultation. The developer took residents on site visits to similar projects completed elsewhere. The 'vision' was then turned into a detailed, but still draft, neighbourhood plan. This was generally supported (eg 60% thought the proposed level of redevelopment was 'good'). Further changes were made, eg to car parking proposals, and the final plan was approved in 2004. It is now going through formal stages of planning permission and CPO.

More information: Roy Smith, Manchester City Council r.smith1@manchester.gov.uk

Whitefield, Nelson (EEL)

Pendle BC commissioned The Prince's Foundation to use its 'Enquiry by Design' method to masterplan the Whitefield area, an ethnically-mixed neighbourhood with conservation issues about historically important housing and industrial buildings in a priority HMR area. The exercise took place over five days, with an introductory day being followed by an open, public session and then four days of detailed workshops.

The intensive nature of the event enabled complex issues to be considered with all of the relevant interests 'around the table'. These issues included the facilities needed in the area and, most importantly, how best to balance the unique heritage of the area with the needs of today's community, making it a place where people will choose to live and work. The resulting masterplan was endorsed at the final community event at the end of the process.

More details: the report on the process can be downloaded at
http://www.pendle.gov.uk/site/scripts/download_info.php?fileID=224

Barriers to engagement and overcoming them

What are the obstacles that can be expected? – and how can they be overcome?

Reluctance to get involved

There can be all sorts of reasons for failure to engage in the process – cynicism, anxiety, belief that change will not happen or that decisions have already been made, 'consultation fatigue' caused by failed plans in the past, or people having low self-esteem or not believing they can contribute effectively. Based on the preparatory work in the neighbourhood (see chapter 5), the team should have a good idea of the problems it might face and can try to plan to overcome them – for example, by deliberately addressing issues that it knows are of immediate concern in the area, such as dumped rubbish or graffiti.

People lose interest

Almost inevitably, in a process that can last 1-2 years and perhaps more, the level of local interest will fluctuate, even if there was enthusiastic participation at the beginning. Some ways of sustaining interest are these:

- make sure there are some 'quick wins', especially ones the community have asked for or – even better – gained themselves

- anticipate changes in key personnel – whether in the staff team or among community leaders: aim to bring other people through by training them and giving them experience, in case key people leave or drop out

- avoid endless cycles of meetings, or break them up by varying the approach through study visits, exchanges with other neighbourhood groups, neighbourhood fun days, etc

- try to cater for a variety of interests and make use of local talent – few people want to join committees, but may be happy to organise other local events, prepare publicity, etc

- build on what's there already – 'piggy back' on other meetings in the area to discuss particular issues of interest to that group

- have achievable milestones and celebrate when they are reached

- use a variety of communication methods to excite people's interest – eg making a community video (Hull), creating a DVD that people can see outside the meetings (Blackburn, EEL)

- offer people something in return – such as building capacity in the community by putting on training courses, etc (see chapter 12) or opportunities for people to pursue their own ideas about community events

- ensure feedback on the community's views – for example by getting a senior figure to describe how plans have changed.

Above all, interviews and focus groups for the guide suggested that *slowness in implementing what is agreed through consultation processes* is one of the main reasons that people lose interest.

A specific example of a way of exciting interest is holding a photo competition.

Photo competition in Orchard Park, Hull (GH)

Residents were invited to take photos of their area, join photographic workshops to learn about digital cameras, or go out with a photographer to take pictures of what they liked or didn't like about the area. An exhibition was held of the resultant photos, and people could vote for the favourites, which were then made into postcards and published in a book about the area.

More information: Jacqui.gay@hullcc.gov.uk

Hostility

People in an area may be angry because they perceive their area to have been neglected, or decisions have been taken without consulting them, or a variety of other reasons. The team then has to rebuild trust within the area, aiming to draw a line under (or, if necessary, change) previous decisions and start again. The only real recipe for this is commitment and perseverance – if people in the area do want to see change, they will eventually realise that the only way they can achieve what they want is through collaboration. If enough people are convinced about the legitimacy of the process, they can neutralise those who remain negative or hostile.

In one pathfinder there was discussion in the interviews about the 'blame culture' which exists in some traditionally 'white' communities, and how it was very difficult for the local authority to break this down. Some of the measures noted in chapter 10, on community cohesion, may be useful here.

In Liverpool, a group hostile to demolition lobbied the city council when it was in the process of deciding its plans for the area. To show that the group was a minority, staff very rapidly organised an independent survey of resident opinion over a weekend, and the results showed that the majority favoured the plans.

History of community disillusionment

Perhaps the greatest obstacle is getting people involved, reaching conclusions about what is wanted and within what timescales, then being unable to deliver. Ways of avoiding this include:

- making firm promises only about proposals which are within the team's direct control, or for which resources have already been approved
- being honest about delays and the reasons for them
- if residents want changes to plans, and this will need time, being clear that this is the case so they understand the trade-off they are making
- getting all of the agencies that control resources on board, so they are committed to the same timescales as are agreed with residents
- aiming to carry out two or three projects at the same time, so that if one is delayed the others are still going ahead.

Only certain people get 'engaged'

The team has a profile of the people living and working in the area and should check who is participating against it, so that it knows about particular groups in the community – young people, older people, ethnic minorities, etc – that are under-represented or not taking part. Ways of bridging these gaps are considered in the next section.

Engaging with 'hard-to-reach' groups

Ways of adapting the engagement process so as to be as open as possible include:

- being flexible about the times/places at which meetings are held

- holding smaller meetings in people's houses (as in Fir Vale, Sheffield)

- having meetings aimed at particular groups, eg women, young people

- using unusual ways of attracting people to events (in Walker, BNG, a town crier was used to call people out to meetings)

- going to meet people at the places where *they* meet – MSP has collected people's opinions by talking to them as they come of the local mosque on Fridays (this may work better in contacting men than women); in Burnley, efforts were made to engage men in traditionally 'white' areas by having discussions in local pubs)

- ensuring that appropriate meetings have interpreter facilities and considering ways to make best use of them (eg breaking into small groups)

- providing one-to-one interpreter facilities (MSP has a 'language line' available in 20 different local languages, and also uses an interpreter service provided by the two councils, for face-to-face discussions)

- providing a freephone enquiry line for a fixed period (in Walker, BNG, this was done for five months: 49 calls were received)

- making sure that particular groups are not missed out, eg local businesses and shops, whose owners may not be there for evening meetings.

Specific 'outreach' work designed to engage 'hard-to-reach' groups has taken place in a number of pathfinders. Below is an example from Nelson.

Group sessions in Nelson (EEL)

In Nelson ADF, Social Regeneration Consultants (SRC) ran 15 group sessions during April, 2004, covering about 300 people. Using participatory appraisal methods, informal discussions took place with groups including young people at a Connexions centre, older people at a luncheon club, women at Sure Start sessions and about 50 people from different BME organisations (attending focus group sessions). The different sessions showed the range of views about the area, and points of agreement, between different groups. A report was compiled detailing the views expressed.

Similar work was carried out in Hull. The lessons from the outreach sessions were:

- Many of the issues which come out of specific sessions with groups like these, who might not speak out at public meetings, were different from those raised in mainstream consultations – or gave a different perspective on the same issue (eg community safety).

- Acting without getting the views of these groups would be counterproductive and may well lead to solutions which would not work.

- At the same time, reconciling the views of different groups and achieving workable, compromise proposals is clearly a challenge, given the differences of view as to how problems should be tackled.

Chapter 10 deals with issues of community cohesion in regeneration and how they can be tackled, as they can also be an obstacle to engagement.

[Standard 3.2]

Work with specific groups

Several pathfinders or their partners have carried out specific engagement exercises with schools, often covering all the schools serving a particular neighbourhood. Fewer have done so with local businesses and private landlords, even though they may have as strong a commitment to the neighbourhood (or perhaps stronger, compared with many private tenants). There is guidance on engaging with stakeholders other than residents (landlords, local businesses, etc) in the *Neighbourhood Renewal Assessment Guidance Manual*, section 5.

Fun session at Bradley Primary School (EEL)

Fifty year six pupils took part in a fun session lasting roughly one and a half hours. The children were asked to draw a picture of their street, and while doing that they were encouraged to think about three things they like and dislike about their street and what changes or improvements they would like to see. The likes, dislikes and changes were then written on colour co-ordinated post-it notes and then stuck onto a chart drawn on flip chart paper. The comments were then analysed and recorded. The top three things pupils liked about the area were that there are places to play, good street lighting and good local shops. Top dislikes were rubbish in the street, dog fouling and living near a busy road.

Focus groups with local businesses, Walker (BNG)

Businesses were invited to two focus groups run by SRC. Out of over 600, 35 people came, which shows the difficulty in this kind of engagement. Among their concerns were that the city council produces a 'promise' for businesses similar to the one it had produced for residents, and that they engage in regular consultation as plans developed for the area. They were especially concerned about relocation arrangements and compensation in the event of any demolition taking place.

More information: Andy Eastwood, Community Engagement Manager, on 0191 263 4826 or 0191 262 8980 or email andrew.eastwood@placesforpeople.co.uk

Landlord views in a non-pathfinder area

Although there was no specific event or exercise for landlords in Middlesbrough's Older Housing Study, a number joined neighbourhood drop-in sessions and 53 contacted the council directly to find out about the council's plans. They had concerns about the modernisation of properties, valuation issues if demolition took place, and how the plans would affect their investment. As a result, the council considered setting up a landlords' forum.

The importance of engaging with businesses was emphasised in one of the focus groups:

'Local businesses have been excluded from the consultation process. We don't want to see them leave and the major superstores take over. Local business is part of the community.'

Keeping people informed and involved throughout the process

From the examples above, it is clear that proposals do not emerge quickly – for a variety of reasons – and that engagement becomes a kind of extended negotiation with the community over what they want and how this can be translated into practical proposals, often involving rounds of wider consultation and subsequent revision of the plans (see the Toxteth Street example on page 56).

Keeping people informed and involved normally means circulating information in newsletters, but this is not satisfactory on its own and a range of other methods may be used. Reviewing the newsletters currently used by various pathfinders, a number of 'do's and don'ts' emerge.

Leaflets – do's and don'ts

Do	Don't
✓ have a clear idea of the main items you want to cover	✗ go into unnecessary detail
✓ use images that people will be able to identify easily	✗ have complicated maps or unrealistic 'architect's impressions'
✓ check that the language is easily understood	✗ use jargon (such as 'place making' or 'governance')
✓ aim the leaflet at people who aren't well informed	✗ assume prior knowledge or understanding about what is happening in the area
✓ reflect people's views back to them	✗ forget to make it clear that any proposals are based on local views, and what these are
✓ say how people can find out more, and express their opinions	✗ forget that translations may be needed
✓ keep it short and simple	✗ produce something that requires more than five minutes to read
✓ make sure it is properly distributed	✗ miss people out who can then say they have been left in the dark

---

But other methods are required – even leaflets pushed through every door will only be read by perhaps half the people (or less). All of the pathfinders do, of course, use different methods. Some examples of the varied approaches are:

- *Patch volunteers* – RNS briefs between 20-40 people on a monthly basis in neighbourhoods where major intervention is to take place. The patch volunteers are coordinated by a neighbourhood worker and receive training in issues which they choose – such as setting personal boundaries, maintaining confidentiality, etc.

- *Residents' friends* – RNS maintain a network of independent 'residents' friends' (similar to tenants' friends in stock transfer). They are funded by the pathfinder but appointed by and answerable to the local Citizens Advice Bureau.

- *Implementation groups* – Sheffield run four of these groups in the Fir Vale neighbourhood, covering different issues. They are chaired by elected members, do not have a rigidly-fixed membership but are recognised by the council and have the ability to call in other partners or departments as necessary to work through issues.

- *Community workers* – Sheffield appointed one in the Fir Vale area to help set up and liaise with residents' groups, establish contact with local places of worship, etc.

[Standard 2.2]

Engaging with residents on specific issues

Demolition

To date, about 8,000 houses have been demolished under the HMR programme. Clearly this means that in some neighbourhoods there are significant levels of demolition and difficult decisions as to where to 'draw the line'. Resident involvement in doing this is of paramount importance both in ensuring that the community 'owns' the plans and in demonstrating that this is the case to local councils, the media and pressure groups.

Chapter 7 will deal with the detailed liaison with individual households or groups of households on demolition and rehousing, but the overall decisions about where and how much housing should be demolished, in neighbourhoods with significant problems, is a particularly challenging engagement task. Cole and Flint (whose study was undertaken at the same time as work on the guide) identified[14] four issues about this, from their review of practice in certain pathfinders:

- Residents feeling that, rather than being involved in strategic decisions about demolition, their role has been reduced (perhaps because of time pressures) to one of reacting to decisions that have already been taken.
- The difficulty of gauging whether there is majority support for demolition in areas where opinion is divided.
- The need for communities to build their capacity to engage on these issues, and the difficulty of achieving this given the constraints of time and on revenue funding.
- The difficulty of giving residents precise information about the extent and timing of demolition, given the two-year funding cycle of the HMR programme and other factors such as CPO procedure.

Cole and Flint make a number of recommendations:

- ensuring the substantive, active and continuing involvement of local residents at the earliest stages of the demolition process
- providing accurate, comprehensive and regularly updated information to residents
- respond sensitively and comprehensively to the needs of affected households whilst reaffirming the longer-term benefits to wider communities and neighbourhoods
- utilising a range of consultation and review mechanisms including household surveys, 'Enquiry by Design', 'Planning for Real' and similar exercises to provide residents with the opportunities to influence demolition and CPO areas

14 Cole, I and Flint, J (2007) *Demolition, Relocation and Affordable Rehousing – Lessons from the Housing Market Renewal Pathfinders.* CIH for JRF.

- being willing, where appropriate, to redefine clearance areas and the individual properties subject to CPOs in response to community consultation
- demonstrating that these community engagement mechanisms have resulted in changes where appropriate and that residents are being listened to
- employing consultants or other agencies to build the capacity of local communities to influence decision-making and to improve relations between residents and pathfinder agencies.

The guide adds the following points from experience in particular pathfinders:

- *Be able to explain – in straightforward terms – why demolition may be necessary.*
- *Secure agreement to the* principle *that an area needs radical change –* communities in places such as Sandwell (UL), Wirral (NH) and Hull (GH) agreed that they were 'ready for change' and this paved the way for specific demolition plans.
- *Explain how decisions will be taken and the scope for people to 'have their say'.*
- *Ensure that any tests of opinion are carried out thoroughly, and properly reflect the views of all the people affected* – one of the focus groups for the guide was concerned about decisions being based on votes at public meetings, without it being clear that a vote would be taken and without all affected people being there.
- *Plan for small areas so that people can engage more easily* – Wirral adopted smaller-scale planning areas, getting 'closer' to the community, and this has produced much higher levels of agreement as to what should be done (including demolition).
- *Avoid having demolition proposals 'hanging over people's heads'* – Wirral again has tried to tighten the process so that once agreement has been reached, demolition proceeds quickly and blight is minimised. Residents in Hull want demolition to proceed more quickly and have complained about delays.
- *Put a limit on the amount of change taking place in a short time* – both Wirral and Sandwell had avoided large-scale or multi-phased demolition plans.
- *Be willing to adapt detailed demolition plans in response to the views of individual households* – this is difficult in demolition of terraced blocks, but it should be possible to keep open the possibility of modifying plans in response to one-to-one engagement with householders (Rochdale has done this).
- *Publish a 'residents' charter' setting out principles that will be followed where households are affected by demolition* – Hull has one of these (details in chapter 7) and it includes a promise to make every effort to enable people to stay in the area if they wish to do so.

- *Where possible, have locally-based workers who are independent* – as with the RNS residents' friends (and this conclusion was endorsed during discussions in Liverpool).
- *Recognise that demolition proposals are likely to require a lot of staff time.*

The North Manchester example below illustrates the way that demolition plans were changed at an early stage.

Changed demolition plans in Harpurhey/Lightbowne, North Manchester

At the outset of the planning process a number of sub-neighbourhood areas were termed as 'areas under investigation', which meant that the initial view (based on limited stock condition analysis and market intelligence) was that these areas would require radical solutions (possible demolition and use of CPO powers).

In practice, in a number of cases, a combination of extensive community consultation, more detailed market analysis and more detailed stock condition surveys have led to a much less interventionist approach. For example, in the Baytree Renewal Area, the view of officers was that significant demolition might be the best option but, following detailed discussions with residents, a very successful refurbishment programme was adopted, with only limited demolition. Within three terraced rows, the middle row of poorer quality housing was demolished to create new garden space for the two remaining, which have been externally refurbished and had new roofs provided (including solar panelling which is reducing each resident's annual energy bill, by 20%), street-scaping and environmental works have been carried out. These improvements have been very popular with residents and significantly increase the attractiveness of the area from a market perspective.

More information: Mick McManus, Manchester City Council m.mcmanus@manchester.gov.uk

Thurnscoe illustrates the use of detailed one-to-one surveys of affected houses to obtain precise evidence of support for demolition and information on rehousing needs.

Full resident survey in Reema Estate, Thurnscoe (TSY)

Local authority staff carried out a series of exhibitions for local residents, proposing the demolition and new build option as the way forward for a non-traditional housing estate in Thurnscoe. This was followed up with a 100% door-to-door survey of Reema estate residents to determine the level of support for demolition plans and explain the housing options that would be available to residents.

→

Demolition was recommended as the favoured option, owing to the high cost of improving non-traditional houses to the Decent Homes Standard and the problems associated with the open layout of the estate. All 190 residents were contacted individually (all are LA tenants, with none sold through right to buy). Only two residents were opposed to demolition and redevelopment, which has now been given approval to go ahead.

In Hull, several methods were used to try to ensure a representative outcome from consulting a community about demolition.

Hull's multi-method approach

Opinion on specific plans – including demolition – in three priority neighbourhoods in inner Hull was tested by consultants QA Research, using three different methods to maximise the effectiveness of the survey:

- face-to-face interviews with more than 500 residents affected by proposed demolition
- telephone interviews with more than 800 people, mainly those not affected by demolition
- an 'exit poll' of almost 400 people leaving consultation events held in the areas.

Overall, some 17% of the area's households were surveyed, and high levels of support for the pathfinder plans were identified – including typically more than 80% of residents affected directly by demolition.

A multi-method approach had the advantage of increasing the spread of consultation and making it more likely that 'hard-to-reach' groups would be included. Gateway also asked direct questions (eg about demolition) and this probably made it easier for residents to give a clear response, and also suggests that the findings are more robust than if more general questions had been posed.

[Standards 4.1 and 4.2]

New build proposals

Engaging communities in decisions about new development is often easier in principle than discussing demolition, but needs to be handled carefully so that people are getting accurate representations of what proposals will look like and can therefore comment properly. There is always a danger that commissioned plans from architects (for example) will either give an unrealistic idea of what the development will look like or will be in a form that residents find difficult to understand (or both).

Plans and drawings – do's and don'ts

Do	Don't
✓ have a plan or drawing of the area as it is now, in the same format, so that residents can relate to that first	✗ exaggerate – the purpose of the plan or drawing is to inform, not to 'sell' the scheme
✓ use images that people will be able to identify easily, eg people are depicted that look like local people	✗ allow unrealistic 'architect's impressions' that might be used for a commercial development – this is about people's homes
✓ keep them as simple as possible	
✓ adopt normal language to describe things	✗ use lots of different colours and symbols
✓ check that environmental works such as tree planting or play areas are depicted realistically – is this what they will actually look like?	✗ avoid jargon (examples – 'heritage-led restoration', 'gateway improvements')
	✗ use perspectives or projections that are likely to be unfamiliar to people
✓ check the plans or drawings with some local people before using them more generally – were the impressions they received accurate?	✗ allow the drawings to look as if they are designed to appeal to outsiders – they should be prepared with existing residents in mind

---

Innovate methods of engaging residents in the design process include these:

Visits to new developments, Wirral (NH)

Residents from one area being redeveloped were taken to visit developments already carried out by the same developer (Lovell). Often this meant coachloads of 40 people – there were no restrictions on who could go. After the visits, residents scored the developments they had seen and this influenced the choice of final design.

More information: Nicola Rigby on 0151 691 8249 / 07957 640456

Development partners in East Manchester

In East Manchester, the developer selected worked alongside the Urban Regeneration Company and council and was able to offer residents who were being displaced some real proposals and opportunities to mould and change the future plans. Having a developer partner also meant that the community could work and listen to someone other than the URC or council, giving a level of independence and objectivity.

→

A developer partner can also give options, take residents to completed projects, and raise aspirations. While in East Manchester's experience a developer coming on board was a positive step, it came after considerable preparation. Selecting a developer in advance of a decision to declare an area for demolition, for example, may backfire if residents see it as a 'done deal'.

More information: Roy Smith, Manchester City Council r.smith1@manchester.gov.uk

Other methods include:

- *Capacity building on design issues* – in Hull, half-day or full-day workshops were held for residents to learn more about 'urban design' and 'possibilities planning', with food and drink provided.
- *Design competitions* – Newcastle held a competition between five architects for a new build design for Byker. Residents were able to express their preferences, which were taken into account by a judging panel.
- *Competitions for residents* – such as the 'Dream bedroom' competition for school children in Walker, Newcastle.
- *Helping residents visualise proposals* – for example, the 3D simulations produced on DVD by Blackburn (EEL).
- *Residents have an input to the development brief* – as in the Middlesbrough renewal project.
- *Residents do their own designs* – such as the detailed involvement of local young people in the planning and design of a play and sports area at Bank Top, Blackburn.

Managing neighbourhoods during a process of change

In most regeneration areas, agencies have tackled what might be termed 'low level' issues of managing neighbourhoods – dealing with graffiti, dumped rubbish, abandoned cars, vandalism, empty properties, etc. This might be done by appointing neighbourhood wardens or some similar local arrangement. By having a local person who is responsible for solving basic neighbourhood problems themselves, not only can the job be done more quickly but they become another way of engaging with the community on a day-to-day basis. For example, the neighbourhood warden appointed in Thurnscoe (TSY) was reported to be active in breaking down barriers between young people and older residents, and helping to resolve problems.

A particularly ambitious programme, adapted to the priorities of different neighbourhoods, is 'Living through Change' in Sefton.

'Living through Change' (LTC) programme, Sefton (NH)

LTC is the 'softer side' of regeneration (managing neighbourhoods, environmental projects – graffiti teams, dealing with rubbish dumping, etc). In some areas they have included extra police officers and neighbourhood 'handypersons'. There is a central budget allocated by the pathfinder specifically for these projects, with the aim of supporting the community through transition. LTC money is devolved to the lead RSLs from Sefton MBC, to develop a programme on broad locally-based objectives. The projects are developed based upon priorities identified by the local community.

The Peel/Knowsley area is an example of an area of significant housing market stress, but the impact on the area of LTC has been considerable and there are signs that it has started to have a positive impact on the local housing market.

More information: Danielle Sharp on 0151 285 5193 / 07894 398777

The 'respect' agenda is particularly important to the process of managing change. All of the pathfinders have taken initiatives in this area.[15] One example is from Rochdale (PIA).

Fast Track Burglary Reduction Project, Rochdale

The project was a joint one between the local Victim Support and Witness Service and community safety personnel, and Rochdale Home Improvement Agency (HIA). It enabled the police to provide details to Victim Support of people who had been victims of domestic burglary within the HMR areas. These victims were then contacted by Victim Support to offer a range of services, one of which was additional security measures to their properties. If additional security measures were required, the customer would be referred to the HIA to carry out the works.

More information: 01706 924057

Another example of handling the sometimes lengthy process of engagement in one neighbourhood is from Hull.

---

15 See Housing Market Renewal Pathfinder Chairs (2006) *Transition to Transformation: Housing Market Renewal and our changing communities* (submission to the Comprehensive Spending Review 2007), table 5.1.

Newington and St Andrew's (NaSA) – a community waiting for change

Gateway and its partners were faced with a community losing faith in its regeneration proposals following six years of consultation. Therefore they established a Transitional Neighbourhoods Initiative (TNI) in 2004.

It was essential for Gateway to re-engage residents and two years on significant progress has been made. Eight local volunteers were appointed as Resident Consultants. They were actively involved in decision-making. Consultants helped to shape the future regeneration plans and identify priority interim priorities such as tackling anti-social behaviour.

The NaSA Regeneration Team, in partnership with Hull City Council, has also been important. Open to the public, the team provide the community with information on the regeneration process through one-to-one appointments and meetings with local groups to discuss concerns and answer questions.

Other TNI initiatives have included an event with youth organisations to widen young people's understanding of regeneration issues. This work is to continue through engagement with schools and local groups.

Residents now have a greater understanding with surveys showing 84% support for Gateway's plans for the area.

More information: Jacqui Gay (01482 616268 or Jacqui.gay@hullcc.gov.uk).

Obtaining views on options and final proposals for the neighbourhood

In some neighbourhoods, especially where the proposals involve mainly improving houses and the environment, there may not be a single point at which a 'plan' is put forward or approved. But where significant redevelopment is proposed, normally this is set out in a masterplan. In these cases, most pathfinders have tested opinion on the plan in some way, either by putting forward the options (with the plan being based on the one gaining greatest support) or by some kind of opinion test on the plan itself. Here are some of the techniques used:

- *Surveys* may be used, but will almost certainly need to be supplemented by one of the other methods if a reliable test of opinion is to be obtained. Ideally, they should be filled in by residents, but with help available from staff (including appropriate language skills) if needed.

- *Telephone surveys* help to extend the coverage obtained from door-to-door surveys (used in Hull).

- *Community drop-ins* were used in Hull. Four drop-ins were held in different locations, lasting for several hours each. They included an exhibition showing the proposals for the area, and people could fill in questionnaires giving their views. Over 500 people attended the sessions, about half completing the questionnaires.

- *One-to-one consultations* have been used in Hull and Wirral (NH). These are particularly important where demolition is proposed.

- *Neighbourhood workshops* were held in Bradley (EEL). Options for the area were explained to residents and representatives of local organisations, who then broke into small groups to discuss them and report back on which they favoured.

The range and number of consultation events that might be necessary can be illustrated by reference to Fir Vale, Sheffield.

Range of events in Fir Vale, Sheffield	
Open meetings	23 events; 1500 attendees
Meetings with specific groups	4 events; 100 attendees
Implementation groups	4 events; 103 attendees
Feedback meetings	23 events
One-to-ones	88 cases
Publications, eg leaflets	Six at different times
Written responses – surveys and petitions	986 responses

Recording, learning from and feeding back the results of community engagement

Even in just one neighbourhood, engagement in the varied ways described in this chapter will produce an enormous amount of information – about people's needs, ideas and aspirations. What should be done with it?

The process of recording and 'publicising' people's views is as important as the subsequent decision making and setting of priorities in terms of action. People are much more prepared to accept that their point of view does not prevail if they feel they have at least been given a chance to state it and that they can track a process and reasoned argument in which other people's views do prevail.

Clearly, this will not always be the case – some people will have strong views which are not open to debate. However, thorough and ongoing consultation against a set of core principles and practices, along with absolute transparency and honesty – particularly in terms of sharing ideas they disagree with – are key elements.

The team has to be able to show the range of views they collected and how this was done, the results obtained (qualitative as well as quantitative), the judgement made on the basis of these results and how the final proposals relate back to or build on what residents have said.

If consultants have been involved in doing this, they should be expected to report as fully as possible to the regeneration agency so that they can make the final judgements but also have the material to 'feed back' to residents and others who have expressed views.

It is also very important that the results of engagement are absorbed by all of the agencies contributing to the regeneration of the area. Nothing is more frustrating for residents that to feel they have gone to the trouble of attending meetings or taking part in surveys, only to find that six months later someone is asking for their views again, on the same issues. If this is sometimes necessary – for example, to satisfy legal requirements in the planning process – then the reasons must be clearly explained. It can also be very useful to have a running record of engagement activities in order to meet criticisms from residents, elected members or the press. Liverpool has such a record for Princes Park.

Engagement recorded in the Princes Park area of Liverpool

Liverpool City Council has a documented record of all the engagement that took place in the Princes Park/Welsh Streets area in the period 2003-2006, leading up to decisions on demolition in the area. It includes brief details and the outcomes of meetings that took place, household surveys, newsletters and other events. It enables anyone to see the varied opportunities for people to be involved, the numbers that took part, and the results.

Source: Liverpool CC/New Heartlands *Princes Park Consultation Review 2003-2006.*

Finally, all regeneration agencies are using a variety of methods to engage with people in neighbourhoods, and many different methods have also been discussed here. There should be procedures in place to assess the effectiveness of different approaches, so that the next neighbourhood to be tackled benefits from the agency's experience in the previous one.

[Standard 6.1]

CHAPTER 7

ENGAGING AT THE INDIVIDUAL LEVEL – SUPPORT AND ADVICE SERVICES FOR HOUSEHOLDERS IN REDEVELOPMENT PROJECTS

What this chapter is about

- understanding the impact of redevelopment on individuals
- building resident confidence
- identifying and assessing support needs
- support and advice before and during relocation
- written information
- providing housing choice
- issues about acquisition and compensation
- managing the process of change in the community
- support following the move

Understanding the impact of redevelopment on individuals

For most people, their home meets physical as well as emotional needs and represents the biggest financial investment they will ever make. Residents whose homes are under threat are anxious to ensure that the benefits they value, whether it is their equity stake, location or affordability, are preserved. But older people, for example, may also be worried about the loss of memories which may have greater value to them than facilities provided by a new home. The uncertain nature of a programme and its timescale are frequent causes of anxiety and frustration – including among those who support redevelopment. Residents value certainty not least because it allows them to make decisions about how best to spend their money (eg on redecoration).

Factors influencing whether a household supports demolition include:

- the perceived inconvenience, cost and stress of the move itself
- the degree to which the resident feels in control by being able to influence outcomes and the pace of change
- whether the benefits of living in a particular place are perceived to be adequately compensated or replaced by their new home
- confidence that the programme will be able to deliver these benefits to a clear timescale
- (for older people and those with no long-term plans to stay) the likelihood that they will see the end of the programme and be able to enjoy its full benefits.

This chapter shows how a well-designed support programme can address these issues.

[Standard 4.4]

Building resident confidence – residents' charters

Earlier chapters have described measures to build resident confidence in the wider regeneration programme and vision for the community, for example though site visits and demonstration projects. One way of addressing residents' concerns about the effects of demolition is to provide them with a set of clear, published commitments in a 'charter' or 'promise'.

A charter may apply either to the whole pathfinder or to particular areas. A charter should include commitments to local businesses and voluntary sector organisations not least because they contribute towards sustainability. As a minimum, a charter should set out clearly how residents can complain about the programme, including perceived breaches of the charter, and provide a range of options for making contact. Examples include the Walker Riverside Promise (BNG) and Gateway's residents' charter (see below).

Extract from Gateway residents' charter

- once plans are finalised, individual residents will be informed personally about changes that directly affect them. This will include information and personal support about the choices and help available to them
- every effort will be made to enable residents to stay in their community
- a package of financial help will be available to all residents required to move as part of redevelopment work

→

- residents required to move will be offered a range of housing choices
- all new housing will be of a good standard
- all residents required to move will receive priority for any available council housing
- we will try to ensure that no-one has to move twice

More information: Jacqui.gay@hullcc.gov.uk

Some points about the development of charters are:

- Residents should be involved in their development. A charter which is simply handed down risks reinforcing residents' sense of powerlessness.

- Where a local charter is negotiated for a specific area it is important that decisions are made within the formal governance arrangements to ensure that all partners sign up to it.

- When negotiating a charter, there is a need to be open and honest about what is realistically achievable. For example, a commitment to every resident not to be moved more than once may be impossible to meet (even though it may be feasible for the majority).

- The more specific the commitment the more precise the terms need to be, to avoid misunderstanding and prevent credibility being compromised. For example, residents and officers may have completely different perceptions about what is an 'equivalent home'. To the resident it is likely to mean a property with the same number of rooms and space standards – even if their current home is poorly constructed and they are under-occupying. Likewise to an owner, a rented home may be an inadequate replacement.

[Standard 4.5]

Identifying and assessing individual support needs

Once an area has been identified for redevelopment each householder should be visited and their needs and circumstances initially assessed. The aims are partly to determine what advice and support residents need, and partly to identify what will be required to ensure that redevelopment progresses and is delivered on time and to budget. The interview can provide affected residents with initial advice and information about the process and start to assess their current housing situation and support needs.

People's support needs can be complex and vary considerably. For example, the most vulnerable may already be receiving community care support from social services, others may need help with moving (eg planning the move, making arrangements with utilities, etc), some may just need talking through the process and being provided with a checklist of things to do.

Households who are particularly vulnerable include:[16]

- individuals with no recent experience of moving home (for example older people, or young people leaving home for the first time)
- individuals who are less familiar with housing processes and systems, for example, refugees and asylum seekers
- disabled people and those with support needs
- individuals from BME backgrounds who may face language barriers and feel isolated or unsupported.

Care needs to be taken when assessing the support needs of BME households, in particular those of women which may not be revealed if the head of household is male. Adult women should be offered the opportunity of interview by another woman. However, any approach needs to be handled sensitively and may require the building of trust and confidence first.

Some needs and preferences will be less obvious and/or difficult to uncover, for example because of:

- peer pressure not to move (eg from neighbours opposed to demolition)
- fear that expressing a need will undermine their independence (eg that they will be forced into care or to receive intrusive support)
- failure to acknowledge informal networks (such as family or neighbours) as being support, or simply consider it too trivial to mention to the 'authorities'.

These barriers can usually be overcome by sensitive and skilful interviewing which employs the right mix of open and closed questions. Closed questions are good at gathering basic facts. Open questions help the interviewee feel more in control, allow difficult or embarrassing subjects to be approached sensitively and are good at establishing what really matters: for example, 'what worries you about moving?'.

---

16 This and some of the other lists of considerations in this chapter are based partly on Cole, I and Flint, J (2007) *Demolition, Relocation and Affordable Rehousing – Lessons from the Housing Market Renewal Pathfinders*. CIH for JRF, Coventry. This report looks in detail at the experience of pathfinders in these aspects.

Checklist – points to cover on an initial visit

✓ vulnerability of household members (eg elderly, disabled)

✓ other special needs (eg refugees and other new migrants)

✓ language needs

✓ any cultural needs (eg needing gas cooking/shower)

✓ financial circumstances, such as negative or poor equity, other debts, receipt of social security benefits, other special circumstances such as the need for a for Sharia loan, etc

✓ initial appraisal of housing needs – for example, at one extreme people may be mobile and able to find their own housing or at the other be a long-standing owner, possibly with negative equity

✓ strong preferences (tenure; house type, including size, age and character; location and attachment to their area)

✓ reliance on informal support networks (eg if they have lived in the area for a long time, or a BME household – especially in an area of concentrated BME communities – so that support would be at risk if they move outside)

✓ an idea of how ready they are to move – for example, living in very poor and crowded conditions and eager to move or will resist change and even go right through the CPO procedure, etc

✓ private sector tenants – may be difficult to keep track of them and provide support

✓ early identification of obstacles – such as unclear or unknown owners, abandoned or disputed property, owner in prison or overseas, purchases by a landlord on a speculative basis – where more investigation or enforcement action is needed separately from visiting, and may be time-critical at a later stage in delivering the site for demolition and rebuilding.

[Standard 3.1, 3.2, 4.3]

Support and advice before and during relocation

Pathfinders and their partners have developed a range of services for supporting people through each stage of the development process. These include:

- information about the property acquisition and relocation process
- household financial appraisals
- financial advice and options, use of capital sum derived from sale, compensation rights, equity loans and mortgage options

- advice about housing options including home ownership options and how to access rented housing
- advice about grants and benefits entitlement
- assistance in completing forms and paperwork
- advice about legal rights and accessing solicitors
- advice about utilities suppliers and energy efficiency
- providing information, advice and occasionally practical assistance relating to removals and the moving process
- specialist housing advice (for example on tenants' rights, social landlord allocation systems or sheltered housing for the elderly)
- advice on the valuation of their home
- advice on disability aids and adaptations
- access to social and statutory services.

The kind of intensive support provided is illustrated by The Generation Project.

Individual advocacy and support
The Generation Project, East Manchester

The HMR team referred a couple to the project because they were having their home compulsorily purchased by the council. The couple decided to rent from a housing association outside the local authority area rather than buy another house. The advocacy worker liaised with many agencies on the couple's behalf including: solicitor, surveyor, housing staff, HMR staff, removal firms, utility companies, benefits agencies, etc. The worker obtained the information the couple needed, talked through their options with them and assisted with rehousing. This involved visits to the new area, completing application forms, writing supporting letters and arranging visits. They have now settled into their new home.

Source: Generation Project Annual Review 2005
www.careandrepair-manchester.org.uk

Pathfinders have employed a range of different providers from the statutory, voluntary and private sector. Some pathfinders contract external agencies – which have the advantage that they are more likely to be perceived as fair and impartial (eg The Generation Project) while in others these services are provided in-house by members of a multi-disciplinary team. In some areas (eg Wirral, Barnsley) initial advice and needs assessment is carried out by regeneration staff. This requires the right 'people' skills, and staff with sufficient time to deal with residents sensitively. Another approach is to make use of existing relationships – a good example is the Greets Green Partnership (UL), a New Deal for Communities partnership established and working with residents prior to housing market renewal.

One model which has proved particularly effective is to employ specialist advisers – in Liverpool known as home ownership advisory officers or in Rochdale (PIA) as property advisers (see below). The role requires a broad range of skills and the ability to solve a variety of problems. Liverpool Home Ownership Advisory Service has started a forum to share best practice which now includes advisers from Rochdale and North Staffordshire.

Home Ownership Advisory Officers (HOAOs), Liverpool

The service works exclusively with home owners (because of the large numbers affected in the intervention areas). It is managed on behalf of the city council by the Regenda Housing Group – a major landlord and developer in the city, but not in the intervention areas, a fact which helps build trust with residents. The service is fully funded through the HMR programme.

Initial enquiries can be made either direct to the HOAOs or through the local neighbourhood teams. First contact is made as early as 12 months before any CPO, to find out how residents feel about the process and the area in which they currently live. Each adviser has his/her caseload and will work on a one-to-one basis with each owner-occupier. Officers can be contacted directly on mobile phones, helping to build confidence and a strong relationship with the client.

The main role of the adviser is to obtain information relating to the resident's needs, to act as an intermediary and as far as possible as an advocate on their behalf. Officers do not give legal advice (eg on sale of the home), or valuation, mortgage or other financial advice, but instead have access to a panel of accredited professionals (solicitors, surveyors, independent financial advisers). The adviser's role is also to ensure that the resident has a trouble free and smooth transition from their current home into a replacement home.

To date, the information given in interviews undertaken with owner occupiers has indicated that there are significant proportions of residents who are entitled to disability benefits and care packages but have not claimed them. The HOAOs will carry out income maximisation checks and assist with making claims. Residents often need referral to other agencies such as Citizens Advice or an occupational therapist and the HOAOs will ensure that this is done.

→

Examples of support and services that have been provided include:

- liaising with a family in London for a client with Asperger's syndrome (autism)
- arranging with the fire service to fit a temporary sprinkler system for a schizophrenic client who was liable to start fires
- alerting the police and neighbourhood wardens about the presence of a couple of vulnerable elderly women who had become isolated while waiting to move.

Some residents will require support for a period following the move (eg advice on using the heating system) – the length of time is judged individually but the HOAO's role is geared to ensuring that this 'after service' is delivered.

The Home Ownership Advisory Officers who have been recruited have a diverse range of backgrounds and skills (private sector, advice work, independent financial advice, etc). This has enabled them to draw on each other's expertise to address the problems home owners face within one of the largest renewal area programmes in the country.

Property Advisors, Rochdale (PIA)

The property advisor (PA) 'hand holds' the residents through the rehousing process, signposting options and products and following up to ensure options are explored. When necessary the PA will chase up residents, owners, tenants, lenders, agencies and professionals to ensure that acquisition/relocation is moving forward. The service provides continuity for the resident, authority, housing providers and external services. PAs also ensure that residents are aware of their rights to compensation (home loss, disturbance etc) and are able to seek independent advice from lawyers, financial advisers and surveyors.

PAs provide affected residents with culturally-sensitive practical assistance where required (ie completion of paperwork, contact with solicitors, independent agents, estate agents, social landlords). They act as a 'trouble-shooter' for residents and other parties involved in the process (eg solicitors, estate agents, RSLs, Rochdale ALMO) and keep them informed about the status of the CPO and expected timescales. They also provide residents with practical advice about moving and help make arrangements for the day of the move.

PAs have access to a panel of independent financial advisers (IFAs) vetted by the local authority. They ensure IFAs are fully informed as to the resident's current status and follow up any issues either with the resident or current mortgage lender.

It is inevitable with a programme the size of HMR that some residents may need to be moved more than once. Given the extra stress and inconvenience that this can create, additional support mechanisms and safety nets are needed. Wirral is developing a decanting protocol for the housing associations operating in its area who deliver the programme. Some local authorities involved in regeneration projects provide temporary accommodation in vacant flats in sheltered schemes for elderly residents, which can ensure that they have company at a stressful time.

Maximum flexibility over timing can also help. For example, some pathfinders or their partners allow residents to access their new property before the sale of their own by negotiating with developers, or allow a few days extra time to vacate their home. However these have legal liability implications.

[Standard 4.4]

Written information on demolition and rehousing

All of the pathfinders produce written information including:

- information packs
- newsletters
- leaflets on specific topics (eg compensation and financial support)

Written material helps reinforce face-to-face advice. It can be useful to help reassure the more sceptical or nervous residents because it is perceived as more authoritative and provides a permanent record. Provided it is well written it is also less likely to be distorted than information given verbally.

Resident focus groups can be useful to test out new materials and ensure that they convey the right message. Within local authorities, experience and expertise in producing written materials may lie outside the regeneration team. For example, local authority welfare rights services often have considerable experience of producing written information and will also be able to advise on disseminating information to hard-to-reach groups.

Most pathfinders have developed information packs. These have the advantage that all the information is in one place. However, for more vulnerable residents the sheer quantity of information in a comprehensive pack may prove daunting and it can be difficult to identify which information is relevant at any given point in the process. Ideally the information should be as well-targeted to the individual as possible (eg tenure specific and/or optional material for specific groups such as older people or disabled people). Good examples are from Sheffield and Burnley (EEL).

Sheffield owner occupier's pack

The pack includes:
- a leaflet on housing options which has information on:
  - how to apply for council housing
  - home ownership options of council-owned property (eg homesteading, etc)
  - other low cost home ownership options
- a leaflet on the choice-based letting system (how to bid, etc)
- the latest issue of the newsletter of properties available
- a council housing application form
- a leaflet on compensation and how it is calculated
- compensation claim forms
- a leaflet on other financial assistance such as equity loans.

Burnley's information pack

This is particularly comprehensive. In addition to the above it also includes information on:
- how clearance properties are identified and designated
- CPOs and how to object to them
- other housing agencies in the area including accredited private landlords
- a checklist for moving home
- a complaints form.

Newsletters have the advantage that selected information can be targeted at the appropriate point in the process – such as how to claim compensation. They can also help keep residents informed of progress (such as 'first residents move in') which can help build confidence. A good example of a newsletter is Sandwell's (UL) Housing Fact Sheet series.

Sandwell's Housing Fact Sheet 3, Edith Street Intervention Area

- frequently-asked questions (derived from the home visits)
  - how the land will be developed
  - the process and timetable
  - support for residents
- a summary of the compensation for each type of person affected (owner, landlord, tenant, business)

→

- a summary of the financial support available for those who wish to buy a new home and how it fits with the compensation package
- how compensation and financial support affects social security benefits
- advice on accessing various support services, including counselling, independent advice services (eg Citizens Advice) and neighbourhood wardens
- advice and support for helping to keep the area clean and safe (ASB hotline, stamping out fly-tipping and advice on bogus callers)
- a timetable of events (updated for each Fact Sheet) showing stages completed so far and estimated dates for each landmark
- a simple compulsory purchase flow chart showing each stage
- a photo of the staff team working on the patch and how to contact them.

All affected residents should be provided with a 'moving home' checklist as a minimum. This will help those who do not need intensive support to plan their move in a structured way. Castle Vale Housing Action Trust developed a useful checklist for helping tenants move.[17] It provides a countdown of things to do for up to three weeks before the move to the day of the move, including useful tips about packing and who to notify of the move.

[Standards 2.2, 4.4, 4.6]

Providing housing choice

Providing housing choice for affected residents is not just a question of tenure or property type but could potentially include any aspect that residents value about their home or neighbourhood such as location (wanting to live nearby), or moving to live near to existing neighbours. The pathfinders have developed a range of strategies for broadening resident choice.

Choice in moving: East Thurnscoe, Barnsley

The Thurnscoe village survey revealed strong resident support for redevelopment of the 'bull rings' – four outward-facing squares of houses grouped around a core of enclosed green space. The enclosed area had become overgrown, was used for fly-tipping and infested with vermin. There was strong support for opening up access to these areas so that they could be redeveloped. This requires the demolition of at least four properties in each square – a total of 16 properties to be demolished. →

---

17 Reproduced in Bird, T and Campbell, R (2000) *Decanting Tenants: A Good Practice Guide*. CIH/Housing Corporation. This publication includes a lot of detailed guidance on temporary moves, especially for social sector tenants.

Further consultation took place with each of the 140 affected residents. The results identified who was prepared to sell, and this determined where the access points would be created. Residents were seen on a one-to-one basis because of possible pressure from neighbours not to sell. Thurnscoe is a former coal mining village where many residents have formed strong community ties. Some residents were prepared to move but only if they could continue to live next door to their present neighbours. Commitments were made to move these households together.

To exercise real choice requires not only a range of options but also accurate information about them. Residents may inadvertently limit their choices if they have no direct personal experience of an option and have formed their views from unreliable or biased sources (eg based on the media image of social housing). Some specialist housing options – such as sheltered housing – are often misunderstood by the public (see below). A number of the pathfinders include social housing study tours. The chance to meet people, share their experiences and view the type of housing can encourage people to broaden their options and help shorten the process.

Experience from Liverpool's Home Ownership Advisory Service has shown that residents will often choose a property that does not perfectly match all of their criteria if they are given the opportunity to view it. However, care should be taken to ensure that residents do not feel pressured to accept, just because they have rejected a number of offers.

Improving awareness of housing options available

ERoSH is a national consortium for sheltered housing. Its aim is to increase awareness and understanding of sheltered housing among the 50+ population and thus increase housing choice for older people.

A sheltered housing scheme considered to be 'difficult to let' entered an ERoSH competition to improve awareness of the benefits of sheltered housing. The scheme held an open day for local people (from all tenures) at which the benefits of living in a sheltered scheme (such as a more active social life) were promoted by its own residents. As a direct result applications increased and all the vacancies were filled.

More information: www.shelteredhousing.org

Real choice also requires that options on offer are not unacceptable for cultural reasons, or unaffordable. Examples of options which are culturally-exclusive include financial assistance packages which do not have a Sharia-compliant alternative, or properties without gas cooking or a shower (required by many Asian households).

Greets Green Partnership (UL) has undertaken research to analyse the different cultural attitudes to various tenure and property types. A number of the pathfinders (eg NH and UL) are working with financial institutions to develop Sharia finance options. However, even when these are available, experience has shown that a particular product may not be accepted unless it has been endorsed by the local mosque. It is therefore vital that communities are consulted about the design or selection of financial products.

Particular care needs to be taken when giving advice on loans because in, some circumstances, the owner might be better off taking out a commercial loan, for example if house price inflation outstrips the commercial loan rate. Statements such as 'you cannot be worse off' should be avoided. It is essential that all homeowners have access to advice from a qualified independent financial adviser (IFA). For example Liverpool's Home Ownership Advisory Officers have access to a panel of IFAs.

Checklist of options offering choice to residents

Affordability
- ✓ equity loans including Sharia-compliant finance options
- ✓ new homes grants (Sandwell)
- ✓ low cost home ownership
- ✓ voluntary sales of council-owned property, eg homesteading (Sheffield)
- ✓ home-swap schemes

Awareness of options
- ✓ demonstration projects (Sandwell)
- ✓ study tours (Wirral, Sheffield)
- ✓ meet and visit (eg sheltered housing)

Maintaining community
- ✓ securing groups of property so that residents can move with their neighbours (Barnsley)

Location
- ✓ buying properties in nearby streets (Rochdale)

Property type
- ✓ home-swap schemes (older 'character' properties) (Salford, Wirral)
- ✓ tailor-made solutions through new build briefs (Rochdale)

Tenure
- ✓ allow residents to choose to either buy or rent (the same) new units (Wirral)
- ✓ priority for social sector housing

[Standards 3.1, 4.1, 4.2, 4.3]

Issues about acquisition and compensation

Rights to compensation are set out in legislation. Many authorities have developed their own information leaflets which explain entitlement in plain language. The most helpful include examples of the sorts of items that can be claimed, any specific conditions (eg keeping receipts) and other useful advice such as how compensation affects social security benefits. In some cases work has been done by direct arrangement with local firms to avoid residents having to spend money 'up front' and reclaim it later.

Lack of confidence in the valuation process can cause delay. It is therefore important that the process is transparent and fair. Key principles include:

- No valuation should be carried out without the owner's permission.
- The owner should be provided with clear information about the process and contact details for accessing advice and support from qualified valuers.
- The owner should be encouraged to seek independent advice including an independent valuation.
- All reasonable costs of the process should be met, regardless of whether the sale proceeds.
- Timescales for the process should be clearly set out. The time limits should allow sufficient time to seek independent advice and to consider any offer without feeling unduly rushed or pressured.

Some of the pathfinders use the District Valuer and there is some evidence to suggest that this may help improve residents' confidence in the process. Others such as Gateway and RNS provide residents with access to web-based property valuation systems such as Hometrack. Liverpool's Home Ownership Advisory Officers have access to a panel of independent valuers. The speed and accuracy of their valuations is monitored by New Heartlands.

Hometrack

Hometrack is an internet-based property valuation database covering the whole of Great Britain. Users can find out about property prices in their postcode area for free – or pay a fee for a fuller valuation report on individual properties.

Hometrack uses a computer model to generate the current market value of the property. The model is based on the on-line valuation service currently used by 70% of high street banks and mortgage lenders. The accuracy of each full valuation report is reflected in a confidence level and a corresponding value range.

More information www.hometrack.co.uk

[Standard 4.4]

Managing the process of change in the community

As well as one-to-one support through the relocation process, communities need supporting through the process of change. As people move out, remaining residents will be vulnerable to crime and vandalism if the neighbourhood is not properly managed. Initiatives such as the New Heartlands 'Living through Change' programme (see chapter 6) help to maintain resident confidence in the programme as well as their safety and security.

[Standard 4.4]

Support following the move

The most vulnerable residents may continue to require support following the move (for example, how to operate a new heating system). In deciding the length of ongoing support, cases should be judged according to need.

It is important that the authorities continue to monitor residents' satisfaction with the programme following the move, for example, six or 12 months afterwards. Wirral (NH) carried out a survey of residents re-housed in the Rockferry area and found a 95% satisfaction rate. Such surveys can elicit valuable information as to how the process could be improved in future.

[Standard 6.1]

Checklist for services dealing with demolition and rehousing

- ✓ provide for high levels of face-to-face contact
- ✓ consider intensive one-to-one support packages such as those described
- ✓ consider the option of having independent advocates to act on residents' behalf
- ✓ build the support services around the most vulnerable residents
- ✓ provide residents with early information about the future of their homes
- ✓ following a decision to demolish, provide residents with regular updates and access to a named contact to deal with issues that arise
- ✓ consider a formal 'charter' or 'promise' to affected residents, negotiated with the community
- ✓ have measures in place to provide housing choice in the different senses covered in this chapter
- ✓ provide good quality written information to back up personal contact.

CHAPTER 8

SKILLS FOR COMMUNITY ENGAGEMENT

What this chapter is about

- the skills required
- the need to audit skills
- securing the required skills
- other relevant skills

What skills are needed for community engagement?

Chapter 3 suggested that there is a spectrum of types of engagement, from simply 'informing' people to 'acting together' and 'supporting independent community initiatives'. They require different levels of skill. Any engagement requires communication skills, the more ambitious ones require greater interpersonal skills. This includes the ability to work with groups which initially are very negative, suspicious or disbelieving about what regeneration can achieve. Some people may be vociferous and have previous experience of engaging with authority, while many may be hesitant, inexperienced and difficult to get actively involved.

In addition to the interpersonal skills, engagement in regeneration has its own particular requirements: knowledge of the process and what it can achieve, sufficient knowledge of procedures (CPOs, acquisition, planning processes, etc) to be able to handle questions confidently, and a general knowledge of the council's and other activities within the area.

Below is a checklist of the skills that may be needed by staff delivering regeneration at neighbourhood level. This is an ideal list and not all will be needed for the more basic forms of engagement.

Checklist of skills for community engagement	
Personal skills	
Listening skills	Hear what is said, respond in an encouraging way, record or remember accurately the message being conveyed, check with people that is what they mean
Asking skills	Being able to prompt people to get them to express fully what they want to say; bring people into the discussion who are not taking part
Able to get people to work together	In situations where people's interests may differ, or clashes of opinion occur, being able to motivate people and to steer discussion so that the result is that both or all sides feel that their opinions have been considered
Able to manage emotions	Anticipating that some information may cause emotive reactions, staying calm, and being able to manage conflict and strong emotions and secure a positive outcome
Able to create trust	People often mistrust those in authority, perhaps because of previous experiences, so an ability to create realistic expectations and develop trust is vital
Being able to convey unpopular messages	Whether it is tell a community group that their proposal has been turned down, or telling senior staff that the community is heavily opposed to their plans, there are bound to be unpopular messages
Being outcome-focused	Bear in mind throughout that the reason for engagement is to take forward the regeneration programme, and this requires specific decisions at specific stages in order to meet timetables
Contextual skills and technical knowledge	
Knowledge of the regeneration programme and detailed aspects of how it applies in the area concerned	A consultant, for example, must have a thorough understanding of the local context or be matched with someone who does, if they are to lead on community engagement
Knowledge of the political/ organisational context	Knowing who councillors are and how to deal with them; having an understanding of the relationships with different partners and being confident in dealing with them; knowledge of the roles of local authority departments and how they contribute; understanding how decisions are taken and who takes them →

Contextual skills and technical knowledge – contd.	
Understanding of the agency's or LA's strategy for community engagement	Knowing the limits of what is possible, the extent to which the community can be 'in the driving seat' on issues, is vital in developing and maintaining trust and achieving a successful outcome
Understanding of cultural and diversity issues	Appreciating cultural and ethnic differences, giving the time needed to take them sensitively into account during community engagement, and being able to identify and resolve problems or issues that arise from lack of understanding or from conflict within the community
Basic knowledge of technical processes relevant to engagement	Knowing sufficient about the planning process, CPOs, new development, etc to be able to engage properly with residents in discussing them and appreciate when expert input is required
Knowledge of the context in which regeneration operates	What the current regeneration programme is trying to achieve and how it relates to other regeneration initiatives in the area
Engagement skills	
Able to plan effectively	Preparing properly for meetings is vital – lack of preparation is likely to be obvious and to create mistrust
Able to choose between different methods of engagement and knows how to use them	The different approaches noted in earlier chapters may all be appropriate in different situations; having the confidence to choose between them, and use them, is important
Skill in getting groups to work	Being able to structure discussions, respond to problems, intervene effectively and maintain people's enthusiasm and commitment
Presentational skills	Get across proposals or ideas in a way which people understand; be able to formulate and put forward conclusions or compromises and to sum up discussions
Public speaking skills	Establishing 'presence' and getting messages across effectively, sometimes in a hostile environment
Able to record, feed back and learn from the process	Conveying the messages from engagement to the regeneration agencies involved and also ensuring that they learn from the process

What skills already exist and what are the gaps?

It cannot be assumed that staff have engagement skills just because they have working experience in areas where engagement often takes place. Staff are often wary of community engagement, or may give the impression of having experience when this is not really the case. Ideally, organisations should carry out an audit of skills relating to engagement, designed to identify skills and knowledge of different kinds and different levels.

For example, some staff may have experience of speaking to small groups but not large meetings. Some may have relevant language skills but would need matching with others with wider engagement skills, if they were to take part in engagement activities. Skill in engagement is also something that tends to be independent of seniority in an organisation. More junior staff may have both ability and enthusiasm, more senior staff may be experienced but have 'heard it all before' and have 'engagement fatigue'.

Sheffield's audit of staff regeneration skills

Sheffield City Council's audit was a one-week exercise in which staff were interviewed about their qualifications, background experience and current knowledge on a series of issues relating to regeneration and the handling of major projects. The audit probed their skills in working in multi-disciplinary teams and in briefing and handling the client side when employing consultants and contractors. It led to internal training aimed at filling gaps that had been revealed.

[Standard 5.1]

How are the skills obtained?

Essentially there are seven ways in which this may be done:
- having staff with the right skills already
- utilising staff with some skills, and filling the gaps
- matching staff who have complementary skills, to do certain tasks together
- training staff
- recruiting skilled staff
- procuring the skills, eg by using consultants
- using local skills.

Here are some points about each, based on interviews with the pathfinders and their partners.

Using staff who already have the skills

It is unlikely that many available staff will have the full range of skills, but it is important that some do, especially where there are multiple engagement exercises taking place that are a key element of the programme. It is particularly important to have some senior staff who are skilled and experienced in this area, so that they appreciate the resource commitment involved in community engagement, and the problems and issues that may occur.

Filling gaps in staff skills

A point made in the interviews for the guide is that engagement skills are sometimes available, but in staff who have developed them in a different context, such as tenant participation in housing management. A typical skill or knowledge gap in such a case might be lack of appreciation of how to work with owner-occupiers. Gaps of this kind might be filled by in-house training, working alongside other staff, or exchanges with other agencies.

Matching staff with complementary skills

Typically, this might be a staff member knowing a lot about regeneration as an activity but without the exposure to public meetings and other forms of engagement, being matched with someone with wider engagement skills outside regeneration.

Training staff

In effect this is an extension of the option of filling gaps in staff skills, as it is unlikely that organisations will have the time/resources to train staff who do not have *some* of the key requirements, for example some of the personal skills. Although training courses are available and may be helpful, 'on the job' experience is vital. Ways of doing this are:

- shadowing or mentoring with other experienced staff
- secondments or other partnering arrangements with other organisations
- using consultants, but in a way which creates learning opportunities for in-house staff.

Recruiting skilled staff

This is highly desirable, but difficult, so that retaining staff with the right skills and contextual knowledge becomes very important. In recruitment, thought needs to be given to job/person specifications and to assessment techniques that test the skills required, as conventional interviews will only test some of them.

Regeneration often takes place in ethnically-mixed areas, and so recruiting staff with relevant language skills and cultural understanding is particularly important. Some agencies or their partners have made special efforts to do this, by advertising in community newspapers, securing appropriate staff on secondment from other departments, etc.

Procuring skills

In addition to using consultants, other options are using skills from partner bodies (such as housing associations) which have the right skilled staff from other projects. Using consultants is considered in more detail in the next chapter.

Using local skills

Chapter 12 covers the issue of community capacity building, including ways in which residents have contributed to regeneration at neighbourhood level as volunteers (eg RNS's 'patch volunteers'). One innovation that has been piloted in some neighbourhood renewal projects is 'residents' consultancy', where to residents' own local knowledge is added other skills (through mentoring, training courses, etc) so that they can become part of the skill resource available locally.[18]

Other staff resources that affect community engagement

This chapter has been specifically about the skills needed by those involved in community engagement. But another factor that affects engagement is the shortage of skills or staff time in other areas, which might delay key aspects of the programme and therefore frustrate the community engagement process.

In terms of skills gaps, examples that have been mentioned in the interviews for this guide have been legal and valuation skills in relation to CPOs, planning skills in relation to the relevant aspects of the Local Development Framework, and skills in partnership working in relation to the wider services such as transport, leisure, education and so whose collaboration is needed in developing sustainable communities. Some other skills gaps, such as community architects, are commonly filled by using consultants.

In the pathfinder areas, these wider skills gaps have been addressed by:
- aiming to retain skills, for example by aiming for a steady, limited flow of CPO work, to maintain an in-house team and skills, rather than a heavy peak of work which could not be coped with
- paying for dedicated staff or staff time, eg planning staff
- using outside agencies to employ community-based staff (such as RNS's residents' friends)
- using consultants, but ensuring they have the right community-oriented skills.

---

18 See ODPM (2004) *Residents' Consultancy Pilots: Evaluation Report*.

CHAPTER 9

USING CONSULTANTS AND COMMUNITY ENGAGEMENT

What this chapter is about

- the reasons they might be used
- choosing consultants
- working with consultants

Why use consultants in community engagement?

The previous chapter noted the obvious use of consultants in filling skills gaps within in-house teams. But there are other reasons for using consultants, for example in the pathfinder areas they have been used:

- to make it possible to run complex exercises (eg masterplanning) simultaneously in more than one area
- as 'independent' experts, in cases where perhaps the council is mistrusted or there is a 'history' of negative engagement in the area, possibly because of unpopular demolition proposals
- to take advantage of skills which some consultants have developed from working in other pathfinders, or other regeneration projects, which can bring in new ideas and techniques
- to enable inexperienced staff to learn alongside skilled people.

Points to consider in choosing consultants

The scope of this guide is restricted to matters concerning community engagement, and there are of course other reasons for which consultants might be engaged.

These 'good practice' points therefore cover certain aspects of employing consultants. Many have been identified as a result of interviews for the guide.

Ensure the brief covers community engagement thoroughly

Community engagement is not an 'add on' for the regeneration agency and therefore cannot be for the consultant either. If consultants are being engaged to do technical work (eg design or masterplanning), their brief needs to cover the community engagement requirements in detail, covering issues such as expectations about attending out-of-hours meetings, being willing to adapt plans (perhaps on several occasions) to reflect residents' views, etc.

[Standard 1.3]

If possible, involve the community in appointing the consultants

Wherever possible, it is worth having community representatives on a selection panel or getting potential consultants to do presentations to a residents' meeting before the selection is made. This is likely to require some investment in capacity building (see chapter 12), for example in how to interview and what to ask questions about. Focus groups made the point that their involvement should be as equal partners, not tokenistic.

[Standard 1.4]

Get consultants to convince that they have the skills

If it is clear to the consultants that they are being chosen competitively, and have to convince staff and perhaps residents that they have the skills, they will put more effort into their bid. One pathfinder spoke about a consultant who 'brought their whole team to the interview' and gave the impression they would know what to do from day one.

Consider using intermediaries

If in-house staff do not have the necessary experience to manage consultants, or particular kinds of consultant, perhaps other partners do. For example, RNS used partner housing associations to engage and supervise consultants doing masterplanning.

Choose the right-sized area

Give consultants too wide-ranging a task and they may not perform well. Wirral (NH) found that giving consultants a smaller area of a few hundred houses to engage with in masterplanning was more productive than having areas of several thousand houses.

Do not assume that bigger consultants are better

Especially in the field of community engagement, the staff doing the work should be experienced. Smaller consultants are often in a better position to guarantee that this will be the case.

Talk to other regeneration agencies that have used consultants before

Use the network of regeneration agencies to assess consultants informally beforehand, especially in relation to their community engagement experience.

Points to consider in working with consultants

These points are relevant to the work itself, once the consultant is appointed:

Make sure the organisation has the capacity to manage the consultants

Working with and monitoring consultants, challenging them when required, is a skill in itself. Staff need to have had experience in this themselves, or to be able to shadow others in order to gain it. The number of consultants being used at any one time should not exceed the capacity of the organisation to supervise them and provide adequate liaison. Chapter 8 has an example of a staff skills audit in Sheffield, intended to improve capacity to deal with consultants.

Do not leave consultants on their own

Regeneration staff should accompany the consultant in residents' meetings and similar events. Consultants should have a named point of contact with the in-house team, and (during key phases of the work) probably daily contact with them. It may also be appropriate to encourage contact between councillors and consultants, to improve trust and understanding.

Establish a relationship with the consultant

Once chosen, the consultant is in many ways a part of the team and the closer the working arrangements the less scope there will be for misunderstandings, or conflicting messages being given to residents. Consultants can contribute from their previous experience by challenging the agency's work – this should be encouraged.

Learn from the consultant

If the main reason for having a consultant is to do work that cannot readily be done in-house, important secondary reasons for employing one are to learn from what the consultant does and enable staff to improve their skills by working alongside the consultant. It is worth specifying this in the contract to avoid any doubts on the issue.

Be flexible

Just as community engagement requires flexibility, so does working with a consultant who is part of the process too. Be willing to extend timescales or change the brief if necessary, and keep resources in reserve in case they are needed.

Don't blame the consultant if things go wrong

Whatever action is taken with consultants by the regeneration agency as client, if things go wrong they should not be blamed publicly. The agency has to take the blame, admit the mistakes and correct them.

Make sure the regeneration agency is the 'constant' in the process

In a complex scheme, residents will see staff from different departments and perhaps two or three different consultants. But it should always be clear 'who is in charge' over the course of the programme and whom they need to contact if things go wrong.

Have an exit strategy

Particularly if the consultant is putting in staff time intensively over a period of months, it can suddenly seem as if nothing is happening when they leave. Take account of this in advance by working out how to follow up what they do.

CHAPTER 10

ENGAGEMENT AND COMMUNITY COHESION

What this chapter is about

- why community cohesion is important in regeneration
- opportunities to promote cohesion through regeneration

Why is community cohesion important?

Community cohesion has been an important issue for the HMR pathfinders, and will be for other regeneration agencies, because:[19]

- some are operating in areas where lack of community cohesion has been an important issue in the past (and, in some cases, still is)
- all are dealing with diverse communities, where promoting or maintaining community cohesion is an aim of local and central government policy
- regeneration is likely to lead to significant change, which is both a threat and an opportunity for community relations
- engaging with diverse communities, including trying to reach 'hard-to-reach' groups such as young people, inevitably raises community cohesion issues
- unless regeneration agencies are highly conscious of community cohesion issues, they may trigger unintended consequences – such as replicating existing segregation in newly-built housing.

Given that any regeneration programme is directed at deprived neighbourhoods, it will often include places where the combination of poverty and segregation creates the potential for community cohesion to break down or where issues already exist about

---

19 This chapter does not cover the overall issues about community cohesion, as there is well-established policy material and a growing amount of good practice guidance. See for example, LGA et al (2002) *Guidance on Community Cohesion* and the website for the independent commission chaired by Darra Singh (www.integrationandcohesion.org.uk) where it is publishing its reports.

how one group or community is perceived by another. On the positive side, action by agencies which results in improved community cohesion can count as a 'plus' for the programme.

The government guidance on community cohesion in area-based initiatives suggests a range of issues that may arise, especially at neighbourhood level.

Community cohesion and area-based initiatives – issues and suggested questions

- How well do different groups in the area get on?
- What are the main factors that prevent people from getting on? For example, is it a thematic issue such as housing or education, or a generational issue, or perhaps something related to the history of the area?
- Do people who have recently moved into the area take part in local activities?
- How long do people stay in the area?
- How well are people from different minority ethnic groups and, in particular, asylum seekers and refugees, accepted locally?
- How involved are younger, as well as older, people?
- How involved are women, compared to men?
- Are there certain people, for example those belonging to certain ethnic or faith groups, who do not take part in local activities to the same extent as others?
- Who is actively engaged in local activities?
- Is it mostly people from just one particular neighbourhood, or are local activities open to everyone who may be interested?
- How easy or difficult is it to find out about local activities?

Source: Home Office/ODPM (2004) *Building Community Cohesion into Area-Based Initiatives*.

What opportunities does housing-led regeneration provide?

Almost every aspect of housing-led regeneration provides opportunities to improve community relations (and by the same token, to damage them if things go wrong). Key aspects include:

- understanding neighbourhoods
- community engagement and capacity building

- prioritising action between neighbourhoods
- new build and renovation
- rehousing
- improved management of neighbourhoods
- developing a strategic approach and monitoring outcomes.

These will be dealt with in turn, referring to experience in HMR and elsewhere.

Understanding neighbourhoods

Clearly, finding out about neighbourhoods (see chapter 5) means knowing who lives there, the needs they have and particular factors (like languages spoken in the area) which will have to be taken into account as engagement with the community develops. It is worth bearing in mind that this work might well reveal important changes in the area that were not previously known to – or not quantified by – the local authority. For example, recent migration through acceptance of asylum seekers (perhaps in private rented property), housing of refugees, or movement into the area of people looking for work, may all have changed the nature of the area and have implications for community relations. An example of finding out about community needs, and responding to them, comes from Gateshead.

Gateshead's Orthodox Jewish community

Gateshead has a large Jewish community, particularly living in some of the neighbourhoods where work is taking place under HMR. Gateshead Council has a neighbourhood plan which identifies and responds to a range of needs expressed by the community. These include the need for larger houses in the area, which are now being provided through the HMR programme.

More information: the neighbourhood plan can be downloaded at http://www.gateshead.gov.uk/Building%20and%20Development/Regeneration/nplans.aspx

Part of the task may also be to find out about the extent to which there is cohesion in the community at present. In many cases this will emerge through the use of the less formal methods of engaging with the community discussed earlier. In others, it may be possible to incorporate questions relating to community cohesion in local surveys.

Government guidance on indicators of cohesion includes suggested indicators that can be used or adapted locally, and questions that can be asked in local surveys.[20]

20 Home Office (2003) *Building a Picture of Community Cohesion.*

Questions include asking residents whether their area is one where people from different backgrounds can get on well together, or whether they think they can influence decisions affecting their area. Clearly, questions of this kind, as well as providing useful indicators of community cohesion (especially if compared with other areas), also help in wider understanding of a neighbourhood.

Community engagement and capacity building

Regeneration programmes such as HMR provide a unique opportunity, through engaging with diverse communities, to promote greater cohesion. For example, part of the official definition of community cohesion includes having a 'common vision and sense of belonging',[21] which in practice is difficult to develop across a whole town or city. But in a neighbourhood where detailed engagement is taking place, with the aim of developing consensus on how the neighbourhood should be improved, a 'common vision' becomes a practical possibility or even a necessity. In interviews in Burnley, local authority staff commented on the shared issues between different ethnic groups in a neighbourhood, and how the realisation that issues were shared helped in sustaining community cohesion.

Also, because of the changes that any regeneration programme is likely to bring about, different groups within the community can be encouraged (or may in any case take the opportunity) to use the change which the area faces, to have more contact with each other through residents' meetings and to 'join forces' to put their case to the regeneration agency or local authority in ways which may not have occurred before.

As discussed in chapter 6, one aim of community engagement is to reach people within the community who otherwise might not readily attend meetings or may be marginalised from the decision-making process. There are several dimensions to this work which relate to community cohesion. Some possible examples are:

- work with schools to find out students' attitudes to their area, which may well throw light on relations between different groups within the area, that can then be followed up
- meetings with 'hard-to-reach' groups such as asylum seekers and refugees, which may give a voice to people not usually heard, and raise issues which are different from those raised by other sections of the community
- efforts to engage with ethnic minority women may provide opportunities to create links with other women in the community, if they do not already exist.

Community capacity building work offers particular opportunities. An example (from outside the HMR programme) is provided by Burnley.

---

21 See the LGA guidance cited earlier.

Capacity building in Burnley

Following the disturbances in Burnley in the summer of 2001, the Neighbourhood Renewal Unit (NRU) established the Community Facilitation Programme (CFP) to reduce inter-ethnic community conflict in high risk areas by:

- improving intelligence gathering
- undertaking conflict resolution and prevention work where tensions were identified
- strengthening conflict resolution capacity and
- removing barriers to the implementation of neighbourhood renewal.

As part of the CFP, the NRU commissioned two conflict resolution advisers to undertake a scoping exercise and to develop a proposal to build local capacity for conflict resolution and mediation at the community level in Burnley. The Burnley Community Facilitation Project emerged from this process. Its aims were to develop and train mediation and conflict resolution specialists, to develop the community mediation service, to develop local facilitation networks and provide training to local facilitators.

The trainees found the training useful, the series of town meetings took place and the network of facilitators was successfully formed. The challenge is to sustain the work by identifying funding for the future.

Source: www.renewal.net *Training Community Facilitators in Burnley.*

Within the HMR programme in Burnley (EEL), survey work at neighbourhood level has been carried out by trained local residents (as is the case in some other pathfinders), and this was reported as being particularly beneficial to community relations.

Prioritising action between neighbourhoods

One area of potential difficulty, in any programme which involves prioritising neighbourhoods, is the perception that an area which is primarily lived in by one ethnic group is being given preference over another, simply because of ethnic differences. If this problem arises, it should be tackled and not ignored. In Burnley, the local authority has worked in non-priority areas, including rural parishes, to explain the nature of the programme and deal with criticisms that particular areas are being favoured. It has even organised visits so that people unfamiliar with the high priority areas can see for themselves the problems being faced. In Nelson (EEL), the local authority has carried out less intensive action in some neighbourhoods to respond to potential criticisms that they are being ignored and other areas are being favoured.

New build and renovation

Both new build and renovation provide the opportunity to reconfigure the stock to make it more relevant to local needs, to widen the housing opportunities available, to attract newcomers to an area and to break down segregation. Some pathfinders such as UL have responded to local demands by 'deconverting' large, multi-occupied Victorian houses to provide larger family accommodation for sale or rent.

There are examples from Rochdale and Oldham of ways in which new development has been used to create more mixed communities, involving considerable community engagement to achieve the desired outcome. In Burnley, in an ethnically-mixed area facing demolition, rehousing is being arranged (in agreement with the community) in a way which preserves this mix.

New development aids cohesion in Rochdale and Oldham

In Rochdale, the earlier Canalside Community Induction Project was aimed at ensuring the success of a new development, aimed particularly at alleviating overcrowding among Bangladeshi households, which was built on a brownfield site outside the 'traditional' Bangladeshi area. The project ran for three years from 2001 and was judged successful.

St Mary's Partnership in Oldham (formed by First Choice Homes and Portico HA) had similar aims, relating to planned new build on an existing, traditionally 'white' estate. The partnership worked with existing and potential residents, was community-based, recruited local people and worked in a variety of different ways, eg by organising activities for children and young people.

Sources: the Rochdale project and the follow up Community Induction Project (see below) are reported in *How Housing Management can Contribute to Community Cohesion* (CIH, 2004). The Oldham project is described at www.renewal.net *St Mary's Partnership – Oldham*.

Given that many regeneration projects involve new housing building, and there is usually discussion with local communities about what kind of housing should be built, the questions about its impact on community cohesion (see end of this section) need to be asked at an early stage. For example, as well as taking account of existing residents' needs, regeneration agencies will probably be hoping to attract new residents to the area – and it is important that this is not done in a way which creates resentment against the 'newcomers' which could provoke divisions between them and the current residents.

Rehousing

In most regeneration schemes some rehousing is taking place because of demolition or to alleviate overcrowding. Whether rehousing is in purpose-built accommodation, or in the existing stock, it provides an opportunity both to meet the housing aspirations of the households concerned and to create more mixed communities. Work is likely to take place to find out the aspirations of those likely to move. In some cases there will be a strong desire to stay in the existing community, but in others people might aspire to change.

A detailed study of housing aspirations among different South Asian groups in Bradford, for example, found that while many older people want to stay in established communities, some younger people would prefer to move away, if housing opportunities were available that are not too far away from 'traditional' Asian areas.[22]

However, this raises the possible need to support BME residents in making such moves. Rochdale's Community Induction Project is doing that.

Rochdale's Community Induction Project (CIP)

CIP is aimed at supporting moves by Asian households into social rented housing near to, but not within, the 'traditional' Asian areas. CIP operates in both Rochdale and Oldham. CIP consists of a small team of officers (predominately from BME communities) working mainly with RSL and ALMO tenants and waiting list applicants with housing need, which cannot be satisfied within their first choice area. The aim of the service is to encourage applicants to consider non-traditional areas of social housing where there is less pressure on the housing stock. This has involved considerable support of 150 residents, both pre- and post-move, multiple visits and working with landlords to solve problems (including racial harassment).

Source: *How Housing Management can Contribute to Community Cohesion* (CIH, 2004).

Improved management of neighbourhoods

Improving the management of neighbourhoods enables problems to be tackled – such as vandalism and anti-social behaviour – which are often particular deterrents to their becoming more mixed. Tackling such problems also provides opportunities for people to work together in agreeing priorities, and even to work practically in clearing rubbish or tackling problem sites.

---

22 Ratcliffe, P et al (2001) *Breaking Down the Barriers: Improving Asian Access to Social Rented Housing*. CIH for Bradford City Council.

An example of a way to get diverse groups to discuss and agree on neighbourhood priorities is provided by Bolton.

Bolton community-based drama

Hact (Housing Associations Charitable Trust) has a project – Communities R Us – which is promoting contact at neighbourhood level between different communities, focussing on areas where there has been recent migration.

In Bolton, one aspect of the project has been a community-based drama. The drama provided the catalyst for discussion, which may help to realise aspirations and resolve problems within the area. Painstaking door-to-door consultation provided material, with actors recruited from the neighbourhood, to 'play back' opinions about the area in a way which provoked discussion and helped to demonstrate that concerns are shared. The drama was organised by a local person with experience in this field.

The drama consisted of eight sketches. The actors were Somali, Indian Hindu, Muslim Asian and Kurdish. The sketches mainly relied on mime and were watched by over 100 people. The audience clearly found it thought provoking and interesting. Discussion afterwards led to several positive comments about improving the area and to some active discussions between members of the three main resident groups (white, Asian and refugees). A follow up meeting has decided that it is a priority to hold more shared events.

More information about Communities R Us: www.hact.org.uk

A strategic approach and monitoring outcomes

Community cohesion should be a factor in deciding courses of action and in monitoring the impact of regeneration. Agencies should be asking questions such as:

- will this help or hinder community cohesion?
- what will the impact be?
- should there be an overall strategy for community cohesion within the regeneration programme?
- do we have ways of measuring whether objectives are being met?

Urban Living has responded to criticisms of its programme by developing a specific component addressing community cohesion issues.

Urban Living's draft community cohesion action plan

The aim of the plan is to ensure that community cohesion principles are at the heart of the pathfinder's work. There is a specific sub-group charged with developing and implementing the plan, based on an 'agenda' of what community cohesion means in the pathfinder area. The draft includes 19 actions aimed at addressing cohesion issues in the HMR work, and two at improving the extent to which UL and its delivery agents are representative of the local community.

UL has also set up a 'virtual' panel of about 800 people in various communities, contactable by phone or email, who act as a sounding board for new actions in this area.

Possible indicators and how to use them are considered in *Building a Picture of Community Cohesion* (Home Office, 2003). An example of their use is provided by Rochdale and Oldham.

Measuring community cohesion in Rochdale and Oldham

Rochdale and Oldham carried out a survey to find out how residents felt about a number of issues. The questions included some designed to measure community cohesion: respondents were asked to rate how far they agreed or disagreed with statements such as *'I feel safe in my area'* and *'the local area is a place where people from different backgrounds get on well together'*.

There were 33,000 responses to the survey, which means that the data are robust enough to provide a benchmark for individual neighbourhoods. The survey will be repeated every two years to track changes in community cohesion. Participation levels in community events are also measured and ethnic monitoring of tenants of new developments is carried out.

Source: Home Office/ODPM (2004) *Building Community Cohesion into Area-Based Initiatives*.

The changes being brought about by regeneration need to be seen against the background of wider work on community cohesion that is taking place in many areas. Will regeneration contribute positively to that work? Are those taking the lead on community cohesion generally aware of and involved in the regeneration programme? Might the investment in particular areas bring charges of favouritism towards those areas? How will this be addressed? The actions which the regeneration agencies are taking provide an immense opportunity – but also a risk – in working towards community cohesion objectives.

[Standard 3.3]

CHAPTER 11

FORMAL ENGAGEMENT IN THE PLANNING PROCESS

What this chapter is about

- the statutory planning process
- the key elements
- other 'plans' within housing-led regeneration
- formal consultation requirements and how they relate to community engagement in regeneration

What is the statutory planning process?

The statutory responsibility for planning rests with the local planning authority – which in a two-tier system is the district council (although with the county council also having various planning powers). The planning authority both prepares and implements plans (see page 110), and controls development through planning applications.

Statutory plans are, of course, not the only ones which local authorities prepare, but other types of plan (see below) can be treated as 'material' to the statutory plans where this is appropriate. For example, proposals to renovate existing housing do not have to form part of statutory plans, but they may be taken into account in them as 'material considerations'.

What are the key elements of the process?

All local planning authorities are now required to develop a Local Development Framework (LDF). This requirement was introduced in the Planning and Compulsory Purchase Act 2004. The LDF replaces Local Development Plans (LDPs) and Unitary

Development Plans (UDPs). Many authorities are still in the process of compiling their LDF so development decisions may still be guided by policies in LDPs or UDPs which are several years old.

The LDF sets out in the form of a 'portfolio' the development plan documents (DPDs) which collectively deliver the planning strategy for the whole area. Two of the documents that must form part of the portfolio are of interest here:

- *Local Development Scheme (LDS)*. The LDS is a public 'project plan' identifying which local development documents will be produced, in what order and when. The LDS acts as the starting point for the community and stakeholders to find out about the authority's planning policies. It also outlines the details of and timetable for the production of all documents that make up the LDF over a three-year period.
- *Statement of Community Involvement (SCI)*. The SCI sets out the local authority's commitment to consulting residents and communities in the preparation of planning documents. It is intended to inform people about the methods used in consultation, the timetable and how their views will be considered. A key aim is to ensure that consultation begins at the earliest stage in the preparation of planning documents and that residents are given the maximum opportunity to influence the plan.

One further type of document of importance to housing-led regeneration may also be part of the portfolio:

- *Area Action Plans (AAPs)*. These may be used to set out the detailed proposals for a neighbourhood, or group of neighbourhoods, that emerge from community engagement in regeneration. The AAP focuses on implementation – providing the mechanism for ensuring development of an appropriate scale, mix and quality for key areas of opportunity, change or conservation. AAPs are subject to independent examination.

Stoke-on-Trent's SCI and AAPs

The city council is working closely with RNS to ensure the proposals that are emerging from the pathfinder programme are refined and tested through the statutory planning process. Effectively this means that the work of RNS is informing the production of Local Development Framework plans.

For example, as part of the pathfinder's first phase proposals for regeneration and change in the city, the evidence gathered and consultation undertaken for the masterplanning process will be used to support the production of the Inner Urban Core and Meir AAPs.

→

> The city council will work with RNS and vice versa wherever possible to co-ordinate consultation programmes between the RNS consultation strategy and council SCI protocols to convey the inter-linkage between the two processes. The level and type of consultation undertaken through the masterplanning will also satisfy the statutory obligations up to the stage of pre-submission public participation on the preferred option and proposal document.

What are the requirements for consultation?

The authority has to say how it will consult people in the planning process, in its SCI. But in any event there are statutory requirements relating to DPDs, including AAPs. The local communities and other stakeholders are to be involved from the earliest stages and be given a good opportunity to influence the plan preparation. When draft proposals are ready, the authority must formally publish its preferred options for consultation and must consider representations on them. The draft AAP is published and submitted for public examination (similar to a public inquiry). Representations can be made, to be considered at the examination. Those making representations seeking changes to the AAP will have a right to appear in person at the examination. After the examination, the inspector's report is published.[23]

What other kinds of plan may form part of housing-led regeneration?

The plans mentioned so far are statutory plans under town planning legislation. But 'plans' for an area may take other forms. For example:

- *Area Development Frameworks (ADFs)* accompany housing market renewal prospectuses. They are prepared by the pathfinder or local authority and set out their vision and funding programme for achieving renewal in the different parts of their area. The ADFs translate the overall strategy into actions at the local authority level. For example, in Sheffield, there are three ADFs covering the north, south and east of the city. ADFs are non-statutory.

- *Neighbourhood Renewal Assessments (NRAs)* are part of the statutory process leading to the declaration of a *Renewal Area*, under housing legislation, which also requires authorities to have a *Private Sector Housing Plan*. Consultation and subsequent involvement in the planning of a Renewal Area is statutory. An NRA has its own option appraisal process, essentially relating to decisions on the future of the housing stock itself. Community involvement in the NRA process is not statutory but is regarded as good practice.

---

23 More detail on the process can be found in *Community Involvement in Planning: the Government's Objectives* (ODPM, 2004).

- *Compulsory Purchase Orders (CPOs)* may be needed to acquire land or houses, and may be made under planning or housing legislation (for example, a clearance area). If made under planning legislation, ideally the need for a CPO should be evident from the AAP (if one is available); in any case the CPO case must be consistent with planning requirements.[24] In making the CPO case, reference can be made to community consultation more generally (eg support for demolition in neighbourhood surveys).

In many regeneration areas, communities are involved in 'masterplanning', which is a term used to describe the process for developing detailed proposals for the area, which might then be included in a (statutory) AAP.

How does community involvement in the different processes fit together?

This can be extremely complex because of the competing requirements of the different statutory processes, the wishes of residents themselves and the difficulty of accommodating different timescales. Ideally, in order to reduce consultation fatigue and to produce plans that are consistent with each other, there should be a consultation process meeting all requirements. Here are some of the key considerations and choices at neighbourhood level:

- *Are the proposals to be part of the LDF?* – if so, the community engagement process described in chapters 5 and 6 will need to relate to the steps included in the local authority's SCI. For example, in the Meir area of RNS, residents were involved in producing a masterplan for the area which then became the formal AAP, subject to a public inquiry. The engagement in the masterplanning provided evidence in support of the formal AAP, but the authority still has to go through the stages described in its SCI. On the other hand, in Newcastle (BNG), preparation of the AAP for Benwell and Scotswood is itself the mechanism for community engagement, so there is one process but geared to the AAP timetable.
- *Can the processes be combined?* – to avoid duplication and 'consultation fatigue' it may be possible to combine the masterplanning process with the AAP. The Royal Town Planning Institute's *Guidelines on Effective Community Involvement and Consultation* recommend 'integrating the spatial dimension into consultations organised by other departments and other public services'.[25] Nelson (EEL) aimed to achieve this through their brief for one of their masterplans.

---

24 For further guidance on CPO powers, see ODPM Circular 06/2004
25 Available at http://www.rtpi.org.uk/item/593/23/5/3

Nelson's masterplanning brief

Nelson set a brief for the consultants appointed to prepare the masterplan for the South Valley area of Colne, which specified that it had to be compatible with the statutory planning system. The brief said:

'The masterplan may ultimately become an Area Action Plan (if land use change is necessary) and should be produced in accordance with the Town and Country Planning (Local Development) (England) Regulations 2004. (All applicants must therefore have an understanding of the new planning system including sustainability appraisals, strategic environmental assessments and the minimum consultation requirements.)'

- *Is there to be a CPO for part of the area?* – if so, it is likely that a NRA will be needed (if the CPO is under housing powers in a Renewal Area), or if it is a planning act CPO then it will be advantageous to have reference to it in an AAP. Some local authorities have successfully avoided this issue by acquiring all properties by agreement.

- *Can ADFs be the mechanism by which proposals are developed?* – ADFs are non-statutory plans and are therefore much more flexible than (say) AAPs. Whether they are the best mechanism will depend on factors such as the need (or otherwise) to rely on statutory plans (eg for development control) or the need for statutory backing for a CPO.

- *What are the timescales involved?* – local authorities need to plan carefully the timescales involved in statutory processes, having regard both to internal factors such as staffing resources and to external factors such as the waiting time for public inquiries. Some authorities have dedicated staff, eg for LDF work related to the HMR programme, or for legal work relating to CPOs. Where staff are accustomed to a particular procedure (eg NRA), then this may indicate a simpler route to achieving a plan capable of implementation than using an unfamiliar procedure which might take more time.

[Standard 2.4]

CHAPTER 12

COMMUNITY CAPACITY BUILDING

What this chapter is about

- what capacity building means
- types of community capacity that are relevant
- examples of capacity building
- important factors to bear in mind
- sources of ideas, further information and funding

What is capacity building?

Community capacity building is defined by government[26] as 'activities, resources and support that strengthen the skills, abilities and confidence of people and community groups to take effective action and leading roles in the development of their communities.'

In reality there is a spectrum of activities that might be called 'capacity building', from modest responses to requests from community groups (eg for a room for regular meetings), to much more ambitious aims of helping established groups develop their skills so that they can become local service providers (as part of the government agenda to develop the 'third sector' in service delivery).

In general, the greater the degree of engagement, especially if regeneration activity moves beyond consultation to 'deciding together', 'acting together' or 'supporting independent community initiatives' (see chapter 3), the greater the demands this places on the community. To participate effectively, people will need to feel confident and skilled enough to do so. In the focus groups for this guide, residents mentioned that capacity building does reduce their sense of powerlessness over what is happening.

---

26 Home Office (2004) *Firm Foundations*.

They felt that it helped them to be more positively involved rather than just having things done to them.

This chapter cannot be exhaustive in describing all the ways in which community groups might want to build their capacities, nor of all the ways in which agencies might want to assist them. The aim is to provide some pointers as to the types of capacity building which might be particularly relevant to housing-led regeneration, an indication of ways in which it might be carried out, and sources of further information or support.

What kinds of community capacity might be especially relevant to housing-led regeneration?

Identifying areas in which communities or community groups want to develop their capacity is inevitably a shared agenda between the groups concerned and the regeneration agencies. Obviously, building capacity starts with the community recognising that there are gaps in what it can do that it would like to fill, and with the willingness of the agency to help it fill those gaps. There are six kinds of capacity building that are most likely to arise in the context of HMR and other housing-led regeneration:

- *programme-related capacities* – such as understanding plans, knowing about different new build options, etc
- *general community skill levels* – such as computing or telephone skills
- *organisational capacity as community groups* – such as governance issues, running meetings effectively, learning new publicity methods, skills in negotiation and influencing others, how to deal with the media, etc
- *capacity to deal with particular issues within the community* – such as community cohesion issues or problems like ASB
- *capacity building in response to locally-expressed needs* – for example, a community group might want to develop a local football team and this might be thought beneficial to the community more generally, and therefore worth supporting
- *capacity to develop community-based services and have community-owned assets* – such as a local community advice centre or neighbourhood newspaper (or even, for established groups, to develop further so they can bid to deliver commissioned services as part of the 'third sector').

There are examples of groups developing their capacities in these different ways from within the HMR programme and from elsewhere.

Capacity building examples	
programme-related capacities	RNS trains 'patch volunteers' who maintain contact with people about the HMR programme and receive monthly briefings. Wirral established a course, 'Introduction to Regeneration' for young people doing access to employment training. The course covered regeneration issues generally, but also had participative exercises covering a 'problem estate' and the question of whether or not to demolish houses. Feedback from the course was very positive and follow-up opportunities are being considered. In Fir Vale, Sheffield, residents carried out surveys in the area themselves, which helped to achieve 'ownership' of the results.
general community skill levels	Freebridge Community Housing (a stock transfer HA) set up extensive courses at a low cost for residents in skills such as using email and the internet effectively, writing letters and reports, effective text messaging and good telephone communications. In Wirral, the Community Art Regeneration Project involved local residents in Tranmere producing artwork relevant to the area, with themes such as community spirit, local history and the future. These pieces of artwork were then reproduced and mounted on selected street lamps along the Old Chester Road corridor in lower Tranmere, an area of concentrated HMR regeneration activity in the neighbourhood.
organisational capacity as community groups	Hull provided residents with resources to make their own community video, to draw attention to the area's problems and enable residents to express their views. Training residents in a new technique helped to overcome 'consultation fatigue' and promote more active engagement.
capacity to address particular issues within the community	The Positive Action Steering Group in Greets Green, Sandwell (UL) focuses on raising the skill levels of people from different BME groups within the area who have been under-represented in community involvement in the past. It has dealt with issues such as poor access to mainstream agencies, the need to improve outside awareness of their needs and the need for internal capacity building, training and organisational support. 'Maker Safer Places' is a project which has worked with women in an estate in Manchester (and two other cities) to help them gain skills and confidence to identify what makes their area 'unsafe' and how to formulate recommendations to raise the levels of safety and reduce fear of crime. →

capacity building in response to locally-expressed needs	Sheffield provided funding to local groups to enter the annual 'Sheffield in Bloom' competition.
capacity to develop community-based services or assets	Sheffield has many examples of refugee and migrant community groups which run services commissioned from public bodies, eg mental health support by a Somali group called MAAN from SP funding; employment training by NETT, a Yemeni/Somali group, funded by Jobcentre Plus. Most received support initially to develop skills such as financial and business management.

How can communities be helped to build their capacity?

There are many different 'ways in' to community capacity building, and this guide can do no more than outline some principles that apply in housing-led regeneration, based on the example of HMR:

- *Organise and build on what exists* – The skills, community structures and resources such as buildings and shared facilities that exist in an area are the basis on which to build and should not be disregarded. The first step is to identify what they are. In some areas, community centres or groups may already exist which can provide a base or skills for capacity building, or could be given resources to do this (see Fir Vale example, below).

- *Consider what social issues in the area need to be tackled through capacity building* – Are there issues which stand in the way of the neighbourhood being sustainable in the longer term? For example, do people relate reasonably well to each other within the area or are there divisions (eg between ethnic groups, between young and old) that are serious and need to be tackled? Does a proportion of the people have links outside the area and with agencies like local government, or do few people have these links/skills?

- *Consider what is needed for the successful regeneration of the area* – The other side of looking at what the community 'brings to the table' is to ask what the regeneration programme 'requires' of the community. Although the guide has just suggested a wide spectrum of capacity-building activities, it could be that a particular area already has the capacity to engage with regeneration, or will need fairly simple measures to close any 'gaps'. It should not be assumed that considerable capacity building is necessarily needed.

- *Ensure appropriate support is available* – Groups may need meeting places locally, seedcorn funding to stimulate grassroots activity, staff with community development skills, access to a forum or network (eg of community groups involved across a regeneration area) and training opportunities. The agency may be able to respond to these needs with relatively small amounts of finance.

- *Work with different parts of the community* – Respond to local circumstances and different levels of need (as in the Greets Green example above). Help people to learn from each other. Build capacity in ways which also serve to make communities more cohesive (eg by bringing people together in tasks or courses who would not otherwise have much contact with each other). Try to 'bring on' a range of people, not just the few who perhaps have always represented the community or come to meetings.

- *Take the risk* – This level of working with communities cannot have a predictable outcome, because to some extent the local people must be in the driving seat. Expect bursts of enthusiastic activity followed by a falling off of interest. One pathfinder found that a locally-based capacity building venture worked well for a period, then losing a key member of staff caused a crisis from which it only recovered with difficulty.

- *Take the long view* – Regeneration aims for long-term change, and community capacity building is a long-term process needing considerable commitment and probably partnership working with other bodies with skills in this area (see below). Agencies may want to work on more than one level with their communities – developing some capacities in the short term to help them engage more effectively with the programme, while investing with others in longer-term capacity building to help to develop a viable, vibrant community that will continue after the programme has ended.

- *Have an 'exit strategy'* – Neighbourhoods will continue long after regeneration finishes, and one objective can be to leave structures in place (eg neighbourhood management forums) that can continue to build on what has been achieved, including the closer involvement of local people with service providers. (This was a point made at one of the focus groups.)

[Standard 7.1]

Fir Vale Vision (FVV), Sheffield

Fir Vale Vision (FVV) is a capacity-building body in the Fir Vale neighbourhood of Sheffield. FVV received a Housing Corporation Community Enabling Training Grant and matched funding from the pathfinder to appoint development workers to build the capacity of residents in the FV area. It aimed to reach 'hard-to-reach' groups such as ethnic minority women and young people partly through the use of more innovative methods of engagement – such as a video project with young people. Through training the residents, they were able to conduct neighbourhood-level surveys themselves.

→

Apart from general capacity building, FVV enabled residents to carry out the survey work to collect opinions about the future of the area, which encouraged participation and gave the results greater credibility.

FVV was enthusiastically supported by residents at the start, but interest subsequently trailed off. When the manager left, recruiting new staff became difficult. The LA had to devote time to supporting the organisation.

More information: Sheffield City Council's East Sheffield Regeneration Team, 0114 256 2182.

Sources of further information or ideas

This chapter is no more than a starting point for looking at how to build community capacity. Below are references to sources of information, support or funding that can help in developing a community capacity building programme.

General information on community capacity building can be found on several government or related websites, for example:

Together We Can website
This website, www.togetherwecan.info, has a range of material on promoting the role of local people in influencing local service delivery. Available on this site is the report *Promoting Effective Citizenship and Community Empowerment* (ODPM, 2006), a guide to methods and resources, with good practice examples. Also available is *The National Framework for Active Learning for Active Citizenship* which has a range of information on capacity building for individuals and groups.

Neighbourhood Renewal Unit (NRU)
The NRU website www.neighbourhood.gov.uk has material on 'resident's consultancy' which looks at using residents' skills to contribute neighbourhood renewal and community-led regeneration. The NRU publication *The Learning Curve* is a training resource for skills development in neighbourhood renewal, including residents but also practitioners. The NRU site also has the government's strategy for engaging with neighbourhood organisations, *Citizen Engagement and Public Services: Why Neighbourhoods Matter*, which has information on support for neighbourhood groups and examples of empowerment at neighbourhood level.

Renewal net
The website www.renewal.net complements the NRU site with good practice material and toolkits, for example on sustaining community involvement.

The government's 'third sector' agenda

The website www.cabinetoffice.gov.uk/thirdsector is a starting point. This has the report *Firm Foundations* and other case study material and links.

Development of social enterprises and community-interest companies

Guidance on the development of community-based businesses is provided by the websites www.socialenterprise.org.uk and www.charityfinance.co.uk/news/117/september2005/cic.asp

Neighbourhood management

Involving communities in managing their own neighbourhoods is one of the themes in *Successful Neighbourhoods – A Good Practice Guide* (new edition, 2007) published by CIH (www.cih.org/publications). It also has sections on capacity building.

Skills and resources for capacity building

Learning from others

An excellent way for small organisations to build their capacity is by learning from similar bodies that have already done so. This may be done in a variety of ways – including visits, exchanges, 'mentoring' or 'shadowing' for key people. Many local authorities have local compacts (see www.thecompact.org.uk) for involving the voluntary sector, and these may cover the issue of capacity building and resources for carrying it out. These may be particularly targeted at BME organisations, under the BME code of practice. One department may have specific responsibility, perhaps with dedicated staff, for dealing with the 'third sector'. The local voluntary service council may also have resources for capacity building.

Consultants

Using consultants with experience in community capacity building can be a good way of bringing in people who already have the skills, and briefing them specifically in the context of the regeneration programme. Many of the practical examples in this guide, involving community participation in options development or other aspects of regeneration, have had a training or development component, using consultants.

Specialist skills or training programmes

Trafford Hall (www.traffordhall.com), TPAS (www.tpas.org.uk), CIH (www.cih.org/education/) and other bodies provide training courses and other resources for residents' groups.

Community Pride

This is a Manchester-Salford group which works on community empowerment issues, including those relating to the HMR programme. It runs free 'schools of participation' for community-based groups, and has skills in helping marginalised groups participate such as disabled people (see www.communitypride.org.uk).

Academy for Sustainable Communities

This is funded by CLG to take forward the Egan Review's recommendation for a new national skills centre to support those working towards sustainable communities. Its purpose is to inspire and enable people across different fields to work together in a coherent, farsighted approach to renewing communities. ASC will work with local government initiatives like the Local Government Leadership Centre and the Planning Advisory Service to deliver on shared priorities. Further information is available at www.ascskills.org.uk.

The ASC is working through CIH to develop the 'Active Learning for Residents' project, through which residents can work towards qualifications in skills in community action (contact: ashraf.ahmed@cih.org).

Developing voluntary sector skills

As part of the 'third sector' agenda, a wide range of material is available on developing skills in the voluntary sector, particularly through ChangeUp (see below). Material on skills for officers of voluntary groups is available at www.hubs.org.uk and on volunteering at www.volunteering.org.uk.

ChangeUp

ChangeUp is a government strategy, with funding of £150m over four years, aimed at improving the capacity of the 'third sector'. From January 2006 it is run by a new organisation called Capacity Builders. Its main role is to create a 'hub' of expertise at national and regional levels (in England), covering the main areas in which capacity building is thought to be needed: infrastructure, governance, workforce skills and performance management. Local 'third sector' infrastructure bodies are drawing up Local Infrastructure Development Plans. Developments can be followed on www.changeup.org.uk, through a quarterly newsletter.

Hact

Hact is developing a Supportive and Inclusive Neighbourhoods programme, to show how partnership approaches within neighbourhoods can help provide a better environment for marginalised people within them, such as those with mental health needs. It has also published *An Opportunity waiting to Happen: Housing Associations as 'Community Anchors'*, which draws on 300 case study examples to show the actual or potential role of HAs in assisting the long-term sustainability of communities (www.hact.org.uk).

CHAPTER *13*

DEALING WITH THE MEDIA

What this chapter is about

- why dealing with the media is important
- what good practice principles should be followed

Why is dealing with the media so important?

It is useful to see the impact of media coverage of housing-led regeneration at three levels, using HMR as the example. First, at neighbourhood level, how the programme is presented in the media is bound to affect local attitudes, especially if a daily newspaper or local newssheet decides to campaign against regeneration plans. Second, at city or strategic level, the programme is likely to be politically sensitive and adverse press comment will make it even more so – and therefore vulnerable to political change. Finally, as all those engaged in HMR know, national commentators and pressure groups have made exaggerated claims about the adverse impact of HMR, especially in relation to the amount of demolition likely to take place and whether it is being carried out in the face of local opposition.[27] All of these can have an effect on the programme at local and at national levels, not least because of the effort needed to rebut inaccurate or hostile stories.

Another, equally important reason for having careful media relations is to do with the objective of housing-led regeneration – to achieve a long-lasting revival in the fortunes of previously declining areas. One of the reasons for an area's decline is likely to be its reputation. Changing the image of the area is mentioned several times in (for example) the recent scheme update for EEL. Turning these perceptions round is not a simple task, and is to do with the reality of conditions in the area as well as how outsiders refer to it. But the way the media present the area is clearly one vital factor.

---

27 See Perry, J, 'Out with the Old' in *Public Finance*, 23 June 2006.

The target audiences for media coverage are just as much potential residents (or people in the wider area generally) as existing residents. At least one pathfinder has been criticised by the Audit Commission for not:

> '...establishing a consistent marketing strategy, finding new opportunities for improving the image of pathfinder areas in the minds of target residents'.

Effective management of media relations is therefore a vital but difficult task. This chapter offers brief guidance on the aspects that relate to community engagement.

[Standard 1.1]

What are the elements of good practice in dealing with the media?

Planning for and resourcing media relations work

Little can be achieved if media relations work is marginalised or dealt with by staff with inadequate skills or insufficient time. Given the scale and importance of the programme, it requires dedicated resources from all of the partners executing the programme in individual areas.

There is a danger that staff working on the ground believe they are 'too busy' to address media relations and communication. This would suggest that the activity is not seen as the core task which, in reality, it should be.

Revised approach to media management in New Heartlands

New Heartlands has changed its approach to media management in response to adverse local press stories about the programme. Appointment of a dedicated media manager has enabled the approach to be more proactive than reactive. There are 'bespoke' communications plans for each major intervention area, reflecting both the overall HMR programme and local proposals. Part of the new effort is devoted to 'place marketing' to change the image of parts of the area which have a poor reputation.

Source: New Heartlands Scheme Update (www.newheartlands.co.uk).

Having clear and shared responsibilities

Media management also requires clear lines of decision-making. For example, in some pathfinder areas it is the LAs who are responsible for media relations. This obviously puts a premium on the ability of those teams to coordinate with each other and get across a common message.

All regeneration agencies are working with a range of partners, including consultants, and all are dealing with elected members and residents groups. It must be assumed that any or all of these may be asked questions by the media or may contact them themselves, and therefore that they should be very clearly aware of the main messages which the agency aims to get across (both generally, and in relation to the particular neighbourhood).

A particularly important aspect of any media strategy is briefing elected members, getting a consensus approach (if possible) about the objectives of regeneration, and getting 'buy in' to the need to change the image of deprived areas. An example was given from one pathfinder of a leading local politician describing one of the neighbourhoods where radical change is taking place as the city's equivalent of 'Sarajevo' – hardly conducive to developing a better image for the area.

Recognising the 'hearts and minds' issues

Because of the scale of change underway, especially in areas where significant demolition is taking place, media relations are part of the process of changing 'hearts and minds' and persuading people of the long-term vision for the area whose price is short-term disruption and change. Regeneration can raise emotive issues that need to be handled with particular care.

One approach to this task is to persuade the media that change is required and that their backing is needed to secure the resources needed to achieve it. In Hull, for example, the press is backing demands for clearance, urging the council to carry it out more quickly so that change that is essential for the area's future can be achieved. Local residents may also want a role in dealing with the media, and this could form part of capacity building (see chapter 12).

To publicise or not to publicise?

The adage about 'any publicity being good publicity' clearly does not always apply as has been demonstrated by the HMR programme. Several pathfinders interviewed for this guide regarded not having been in the national press as a success rather than a failure, given the hostility which some pathfinder programmes have attracted.

One of the key ingredients in avoiding sensationalist or exaggerated reporting is to establish trust (and good channels of communication) with local communities so that they know that if they oppose something their views will be properly heard and taken into account, and that they will gain more by using these channels than they will by making complaints to the press, which may well lead to distorted reporting.

Recognising that 'image' is a lot to do with 'reality'

Regeneration is not a 'product' which people can either buy or reject, and successful media relations depends on real changes in the quality of the environment, brought about by the regeneration programme, which can be used as examples:

- 'quick wins' (see chapter 6) that show the programme's impact in particular areas at an early stage
- high quality design (see the TSY example, below) so that people can see the difference between the programme and previous efforts
- genuine community engagement, so that if the press contact residents there is a good chance that the responses will be positive
- being able to demonstrate that this is the case, by citing the numbers of residents participating in activities or having examples of changes residents have requested or have brought about through their own actions.

TSY promotes high quality design

The promotion of high quality design across the pathfinder includes funding a small specialist team from CABE to work with members of Barnsley's Housing Market Renewal Team, as well as house builders on research and development, contributing to projects so that any property improvements and new build schemes meet CABE's Building for Life standards. CABE have provided local design guidance, are raising awareness and expertise in design within local communities, and assist in marketing a better image for South Yorkshire. The aim is to achieve significantly better quality housing as new build is promoted by the pathfinder, which will be recognised as such by residents and potential residents.

Building relations with local media

The essential message about regeneration is that it is 'good news' for the local area, bringing in unprecedented levels of resources aimed at tackling difficult problems and giving deprived neighbourhoods a new future. Inevitably this means change and some opposition, but focussing only on the negative aspects will be self-defeating. Many local newspaper editors or local radio stations will understand that this is the case if time is taken to explain the programme and listen to their needs in reporting the issues.

For example, in BNG the local media were invited to meet the leader of Gateshead council, were briefed on HMR, and discussed the need for regular stories on its progress. Since then coverage has gradually improved. Another tactic might be to invite the press to tour the area with key people, to be briefed on what is happening. Also, ensure that some staff are trained to do radio and television interviews.

RNS builds relations with local press

In Stoke, RNS set up meetings with local editors and subeditors to brief them about HMR and find out about their needs. As a result, RNS is now more careful about:

- having rules about how to take calls and who responds
- making sure there is out of hours cover
- providing quotes when asked and never giving a 'no comment' response
- having a protocol for press releases
- giving 'early warning' to partners about breaking stories
- knowing and respecting media deadlines.

Recognising the media sensitivity of demolition proposals

Demolition is probably the most newsworthy activity that regeneration agencies engage in, and needs particularly careful handling. Among the points to be borne in mind in any publicity are:

- Putting the programme in perspective – it is a long-term programme, aiming to achieve a radical change in the prospects for the most deprived neighbourhoods.
- Providing balance – demolition is only a small part of the programme; many more houses will be retained and improved, and in any case new, more suitable housing, will be built.
- Emphasising the help available to those affected – the services and products that will offered, if possible with typical worked examples.
- Rehearsing the extent of community engagement in decision-making – with chapter and verse on the arrangements and the levels of involvement, and how they influenced the plans.
- Having 'good news' stories – for example, of people who have already moved.
- Offering to show the media around the area – indicating that there is nothing to hide, and enabling reporters to see for themselves ('would you live here?') the houses to be demolished.
- Having residents who support the programme and are willing to engage with the media – especially if there are vocal opposition groups, getting across the views of the majority is vital.

Liverpool promote positive image for replacement housing

Faced with media criticism of demolition plans in the Welsh Streets area, Liverpool City Council successfully promoted the launch of the redevelopment scheme by publicising favourable views from local residents who had campaigned for redevelopment. This made it difficult for the media to construe the plans negatively. The resultant headline in the Liverpool Echo was 'New Community to rise from the old Welsh Streets'.

See story at: http://icliverpool.icnetwork.co.uk/liverpoolecho/news/echonews/tm_headline= new-community-to-rise-from-the-old-welsh-streets&method=full&objectid=17874714&page= 2&siteid=50061-name_page.html#story_continue

It is vital to plan for adverse reaction to demolition – both to the proposals themselves and to their consequences (eg the effect on an elderly couple of losing their home). This is sufficiently important to have a 'crisis plan' for handling the media in the event that they are suddenly highly interested in a particular story. It is worth discussing in advance what kinds of things might go wrong, how to respond and who should do it, especially outside office hours. (The CLG media toolkit has useful guidance on crisis management in section 7 – see source to checklist below.)

Checklist for dealing with the media

✓ think like a journalist – step into their shoes and walk around
✓ respect deadlines, return phone calls, be honest
✓ be useful – and they'll come back for more
✓ build relationships – trust goes a long way
✓ create a media relations plan, don't leave it to chance
✓ deal in news and stories, not spin
✓ write with accuracy and flair; avoid jargon, acronyms and hyperbole
✓ news is about people not statistics, figures, reports or meetings
✓ ask whether your story passes the 'so what?' test
✓ is there a photo-opportunity?
✓ use all the media – radio, TV, on-line, print, local, specialist and national and community
✓ use all of the tools in the kit – articles, letters, pictures, quotes and interviews
✓ praise good journalism
✓ complain about mistakes and bad journalism – that leads to better journalism
✓ keep a file of positive coverage, spread the good news around your friends and allies.

Source: CLG Neighbourhood Renewal Media and PR Toolkit (downloadable at www.neighbourhood.gov.uk/publications.asp?did=1549).

CIH/TPAS RECOMMENDED STANDARDS FOR COMMUNITY ENGAGEMENT IN THE HMR PROGRAMME

Standard	What this means	A pathfinder delivering an excellent service... NB where an item below is in italics, it is adapted from the Audit Commission's Housing KLOE 5 on resident involvement
1. Residents' views are central to the HMR programme and to the pathfinder's operations	1.1 Residents are aware of the HMR programme and the role of the pathfinder	Has a promotion programme for the HMR, including a distinctive branding for the pathfinder, and checks public awareness of it Has a media strategy which reflects the commitment to community engagement, and how the pathfinder and its partners will handle responses to views about the HMR programme expressed in the media
	1.2 The pathfinder and its partners have an agreed policy towards community engagement	*Has a well-established, effective and comprehensive community engagement statement which shows how responsibilities are allocated between the pathfinder and its partners. The statement is up to date and relevant, and clear as to the aspects of the programme in which residents will be offered opportunities to get engaged* *Has residents who know about, and understand, the pathfinder's policy on community engagement statement and are satisfied with it* *Has local community engagement charters in place and a clear plan for introducing the remainder where residents want them*

Standard	What this means	A pathfinder delivering an excellent service...
	1.3 The HMR programme, its proposals and their implementation take full account of residents' views	*Treats resident involvement as an integrated and important element of the service, designed for the convenience of the service user and not the organisation* *Actively canvasses the views of residents and uses them to review or improve proposals. Residents are consulted and involved in all major decisions that affect the area where they live* Ensures consultants and contractors are fully briefed about their responsibilities to engage with residents, always in liaison with the pathfinder or its partners Removes organisational barriers that prevent effective community engagement
	1.4 The pathfinder builds commitment to the renewal process and 'ownership' of proposals for improving neighbourhoods	Uses ideas and initiatives from residents wherever possible Has imaginative ways of involving residents in decision-making and encouraging them to feel part of the process *Has residents who report a high level of satisfaction with opportunities to inform HMR decision-making and service delivery. Residents feel confident that their input will be valued and acted upon*
	1.5 Proposals for change are based on a firm understanding of the neighbourhoods affected	*Has a clear understanding of local communities within the pathfinder area, using all relevant information, including the input of local partners* Investigates what community groups and networks already exist in an area and establishes links with those Makes use of responses received from residents to build up a picture of community needs and aspirations

Standard	What this means	A pathfinder delivering an excellent service...
	1.6 Residents are regularly updated and provided with feedback when giving their views	Records views expressed and tells residents how their views have influenced decisions
	1.7 Residents are involved in governance of the pathfinder and of the HMR programme	*Has resident board members of the pathfinder who are aware of and understand their responsibilities as directors* *Has set up training for potential board members to widen the scope of possible applicants – makes training and support such as mentoring an integral element of being a resident board member* Has other mechanisms such as resident forums to provide for wider involvement in the HMR programme
2. All residents have full opportunities to be informed, consulted and involved	2.1 Residents have clear routes of access to information and staff	Clear information is available about the HMR programme and proposals for individual neighbourhoods, in forms accessible to residents *Provides a range of ways for residents to contact them – by telephone, in person or electronically – all of which are dealt with efficiently and effectively* *Has staff who all demonstrate user focus and a commitment to resident involvement in their work, and who treat people with respect at all times* *Has front-line staff who demonstrate a wide range of knowledge about the full range of enquiries they receive or know who or how to access the necessary information to help residents* *Has set challenging service standards in conjunction with residents and stakeholders, tailored to meet local need*

Standard	What this means	A pathfinder delivering an excellent service...
	2.2 Residents understand what they can expect through community engagement and both the scope for and limits on influencing change	*Provides written material which give comprehensive information on rights and responsibilities and the ways in which residents can be involved in, and influence, the HMR* *Produces regular newsletters to which residents make a significant contribution in terms of content and style. Their content is up-to-date, user-focused and presented in innovative ways to promote interest*
	2.3 Residents are involved at early stages and have time to influence decisions	*Can show that consultation and involvement always begins at an early stage (for example, in developing proposals for particular neighbourhoods) and that residents' views are taken into account before all key decisions are made*
	2.4 The pathfinder and partners are aware of the danger of 'consultation fatigue' and take steps to avoid it	Engagement takes account of what people have already been asked, views already expressed and the time invested in being 'engaged' Avoids repetition of consultation processes, eg by ensuring that different statutory requirements are met from the outset
	2.5 The level of engage-ment is appropriate to the impact which decisions are likely to have on residents	*Has a range of mechanisms in place that allow residents to participate effectively, in a way and level that suits them, in the design and implementation of neighbourhood-level HMR proposals*
	2.6 Where appropriate, the pathfinder shares power with residents on issues that directly affect them	Creates opportunities for residents to share decision-making (eg in choice of contractors or in designs for new development) *Delivers high-quality, and ongoing, training to facilitate resident involvement in technical matters*

Standard	What this means	A pathfinder delivering an excellent service...
3. Methods used meet the needs of diverse communities	3.1 Efforts are made to identify and involve every part of the community, with measures tailored to the needs of different groups	*Knows, records and monitors information about the ethnicity, vulnerability and disability of residents and uses it to inform proposals and prioritise resources* *Provides information about HMR proposals in a comprehensive range of languages and formats appropriate to residents' needs eg, large print, Braille, other languages, etc* *Works with its component communities to ensure fair representation within the HMR programme* *Works alongside residents to decide the best ways of involving them depending on their circumstances* *Has mechanisms that facilitate involvement of residents that are representative of the communities within the pathfinder area* Always has interpreter/translation facilities available where appropriate, even if on some occasions they are not used *Does not discriminate against any person or other organisation on the grounds of race, ethnic origin, disability, nationality, gender, sexuality, age, class, appearance, religion, responsibility for dependants, unrelated criminal activities, being HIV positive or having AIDS, or any other matter which causes a person to be treated with injustice*
	3.2 Special and imaginative efforts are made to identify and involve 'hard-to-reach' groups	*Can demonstrate how the varied methods of resident involvement have led to black and minority ethnic (BME) and hard-to-engage groups having an impact on the HMR programme* *Provides a range of support to enable residents with specific needs to be involved, for example by offering travel or carers' allowances, using accessible venues for meetings, translating information, providing hearing loop systems, visiting housebound residents at home, etc*

Standard	What this means	A pathfinder delivering an excellent service...
	3.3 Achieving community cohesion is a key consideration in engaging with residents	Has a strategy for promoting community cohesion through the HMR programme and links with other agencies to achieve its objectives
4. Delivery of the programme takes account of residents' needs in areas where intensive changes are taking place	4.1 In these areas, time is allowed for more intensive and detailed community engagement	As far as possible, takes individual preferences into account in providing new housing, in rehousing arrangements, in phasing redevelopment, etc
	4.2 Residents can challenge proposals that affect them directly	Considers appointing 'residents' friends' or similar arrangements to provide an element of independent support
	4.3 Special efforts are made to identify the support needs of all residents affected by demolition, including residents in 'hard-to-reach' groups	Offers every resident affected by demolition the opportunity of a personal interview in their home
	4.4 Support mechanisms are in place to help people through intensive change	Ensures regular one-to-one communication and easy contact arrangements to deal with problems

Provides good quality written information in the main community languages and in accessible formats explaining financial and other arrangements important to affected households

Financial assistance and support packages are in place which take account of the diverse needs of residents including any cultural preferences |
| | 4.5 Clear promises are made about how major change (eg demolition) will be handled | Develops a local 'charter' or 'promise' in consultation with residents

Carefully manages the process 'on the ground' (eg in dealing with vandalism, empty properties, etc) |

Standard	What this means	A pathfinder delivering an excellent service...
	4.6 Residents understand how to complain if they have problems	Has a complaints mechanism and uses the results to improve the service
5. Adequate resources are provided for community engagement	5.1 Funding and staffing are in place to make effective community engagement happen either through dedicated resources or through the pathfinder's partners or consultants	Reviews the staff skill base of the pathfinder and its partners, and has training in place to improve community engagement skills where necessary *Provides significant resources for resident training, which is developed with residents* *Is aware of, and successfully bids, for appropriate additional resources to deliver community engagement (for example, Housing Corporation grants)*
6. The effects of engaging communities are evaluated and results used to improve the process	6.1 Community engagement is monitored, results are recorded and evaluated against the objectives which have been set	*Collects accurate information on resident involvement costs and benefits and uses it to decide priorities and to strategically manage resources* *Can demonstrate that residents have used training opportunities and/or their skills and abilities to make a real impact on the HMR programme* *Has delivered improvements to the HMR programme as a result of community engagement* *Consistently meets or exceeds targets and performance indicators on community engagement*
7. The time-limited nature of the programme is recognised; measures are taken to ensure that community engage-ment continues and is sustainable	7.1 Capacity is developed within the community so that it can sustain community-led organisations into the future	Fosters community-led organisations intended to outlast the HMR programme and make a permanent improvement in the life of the community *Can demonstrate links between resident involvement and community development and develops projects that promote sustainable communities*

Standard	What this means	A pathfinder delivering an excellent service...
	7.2 The programme is aiming for lasting change in the levels at which communities are engaged with government and with service providers	Is able to show how the pathfinder and its partners have learnt from community engagement and how it has influenced their organisations' policies and practices

BIBLIOGRAPHY

Key published documents used in the Guide

Audit Commission (2005) *Housing Market Renewal* (available at www.audit-commission.gov.uk/reports/NATIONAL-REPORT.asp?CategoryID=&ProdID=184E49B1-6B96-4efc-9D85-A004C6E9E9B0).

CLG (2006) *Strong and Prosperous Communities – The Local Government White Paper* (available at www.communities.gov.uk/index.asp?id=1503999).

Cole, I and Nevin, B (2004), *The Road to Renewal: The early development of the Housing Market Renewal programme in England*, Joseph Rowntree Foundation, York.

Cole, I and Flint, J (2007) *Demolition, Relocation and Affordable Rehousing – Lessons from the Housing Market Renewal Pathfinders*. CIH for JRF.

Dean, J and Hastings, A (2000) *Challenging Images – Housing Estates, Stigma and Deprivation*. JRF, York.

Duncan, P and Thomas, S (2007) *Successful Neighbourhoods: A good practice guide*. CIH, Coventry.

Home Office (2003) *Building a Picture of Community Cohesion* (available at www.communities.gov.uk/index.asp?id=1502689).

Home Office/ODPM (2004) *Building Community Cohesion into Area-Based Initiatives*.

Housing Market Renewal Pathfinder Chairs (2006) *Transition to Transformation: Housing Market Renewal and our changing communities* (available at www.oldhamrochdalehmr.co.uk/publications.htm).

ODPM (2004) *Neighbourhood Renewal Assessment Guidance Manual* (available at www.neighbourhood.gov.uk/publications.asp?did=1540).

ODPM (2004) *Community Involvement in Planning: the Government's Objectives* (available at www.communities.gov.uk/index.asp?id=1505473).

Perry, J, 'Out with the Old' in *Public Finance*, 23 June 2006 (available at www.cipfa.org.uk/publicfinance/features_details.cfm?News_id=27997).

Taylor, M (1992) *Signposts to Community Development.* Community Development Foundation.

Taylor, M (1995) *Unleashing the Potential: Bringing residents to the centre of regeneration.* JRF, York.

Robinson, F (2005) *Regenerating the West End of Newcastle: What went wrong?* (available from www.sustainable-cities.org.uk/Database_files).

Royal Town Planning Institute (2007) *Guidelines on Effective Community Involvement and Consultation* (available at www.rtpi.org.uk/item/593/23/5/3).

Wadhams, C (2006) *An Opportunity Waiting to Happen: Housing Associations as 'Community Anchors'.* Hact/NHF.

Wilcox, D (1994) *Guide to Effective Participation.* JRF, York (out of print, but downloadable at www.partnerships.org.uk).